CRUCIFIED AND RISEN

PLVSIEVRS SERMONS DE IEHAN CALuin

touchant la Diuinite, humanite & natiuite de noſtre Seigneur Ieſus Chriſt: Item touchant ſa paſſion, mort, reſurrection, aſcenſion, & dernier aduenement: Puis touchant la deſcente du S. Eſprit ſur les Apoſtres, & la premiere predication de S. Pierre:

DESQVELS VOVS TROVuerez l'ordre en la page ſuyuante.

Des creux manoirs & pleins d'obſcurite

Dieu par le temps retire Verite.

M. D. LVIII.

De l'imprimerie de Conrad Badius.

AVEC PRIVILEGE.

Title page of the first French edition of Calvin's *Sermons on the Deity, Humanity and Nativity of our Lord Jesus Christ, and likewise on his Passion, Death, Resurrection, Ascension and Last Advent* (Geneva: Conrad Badius, 1558). The legend around the printer's mark reads: 'From empty dwellings full of darkest night, God with Time's help draws Truth into the light.'

CRUCIFIED AND RISEN

Sermons on Matthew 26–28

John Calvin

Newly translated from the French of 1558

by

Robert White

THE BANNER OF TRUTH TRUST

THE BANNER OF TRUTH TRUST

Head Office
3 Murrayfield Road
Edinburgh
EH12 6EL
UK

North America Office
PO Box 621
Carlisle
PA 17013
USA

banneroftruth.org

*

First Banner of Truth edition 2020

First published in French by Conrad Badius, under the title *Plusieurs sermons de Iehan Calvin touchant la divinité, humanité et nativité de nostre Seigneur Iesus Christ*, Geneva, 1558.

First English edition, translated by Thomas Stocker, published by Thomas Dawson for George Bishop, under the title *Divers Sermons of Master Iohn Calvin, concerning the Divinitie, Humanitie and Nativitie of our Lorde Iesus Christe*, London, 1581.

This new translation is based on the French text of 1558 found in *Calvini opera quae supersunt omnia*, ed. G. Baum, E. Cunitz and E. Reuss (Brunswick and Berlin: C.A. Schwetschke & Son, 1863–1900), 46: 829-954.

*

ISBN
Print: 978 1 84871 965 1
Epub: 978 1 84871 966 8
Kindle: 978 1 84871 967 5

*

Typeset in 11/15 pt Adobe Caslon Pro at
The Banner of Truth Trust, Edinburgh

Printed in the USA by
Versa Press, Inc.,
East Peoria, IL

CONTENTS

Through the death of Christ we are blessed, that is, justified and made alive. As long as sin, death and the curse remain in us, sin damns us, death kills us and the curse curses us; but when these things are transferred to Christ, what is ours becomes his, and what is his becomes ours. Let us learn, therefore, in every temptation, to transfer sin, death, the curse and all the evils that oppress us from ourselves to Christ, and on the other hand to transfer righteousness, life and blessing from him to us. For he does in fact bear all our evils, because God the Father, as Isaiah says, 'has laid on him the iniquity of us all.'

LUTHER, *Lectures on Galatians, LW* 26:292.

If we seek for salvation, the name of Jesus alone teaches us that it is in him. ... If we desire the gifts of the Holy Spirit, we will find them in his anointing. If we are looking for strength, we have it in his lordship. ... If we ask for redemption, his passion provides it. In his condemnation we have our absolution. If we want pardon for sin's curse, that gift lies in his cross. Atonement we have in his sacrifice and cleansing in his blood. Our reconciliation was effected by his descent into hell; the mortification of our flesh lies in his burial, and newness of life in his resurrection, through which we also have the hope of immortality.

CALVIN, *Institutes of the Christian Religion*, II.16.19.

INTRODUCTION

Calvin's practice, when preaching to his Genevan congregation, was not to deliver homilies on given themes or on discrete portions of Scripture as had been the custom in the medieval church, but to preach through a whole book at a time, verse by verse, chapter by chapter. In the case of a short book like Joel or Obadiah, a month or two might suffice; in the case of a larger book like Isaiah or Ezekiel, a much longer period, measured in years, was required. Even a relatively modest text of four or five chapters, such as 2 Timothy, which is almost wholly concerned with practical issues, provided material enough to occupy the preacher for four months in the summer of 1555.

From time to time, however, Calvin would suspend his current sermon series in order to focus attention on key dates in the Christian calendar: Christmas, Easter and Pentecost. We know, for example, that between 1549 and 1562 he preached regularly from Luke on the nativity, from Matthew and, less often, from John on Christ's passion, death and resurrection, and from Acts on the descent of the Holy Spirit. A Council ordinance of March 1544 in fact required preachers to 'preach the passion' throughout Holy Week, and what evidence we have shows that the Reformer was happy to comply.[1]

[1] Cf. T. H. L. Parker, *Calvin's Preaching* (Edinburgh: T&T Clark, 1992), pp. 160–62.

Calvin's attitude to the observance of feast days was less strict than is sometimes supposed. Following his return from Strasbourg to Geneva in 1541, he made no attempt to press for the abolition of the established feast days of Christmas, Circumcision, Annunciation and Ascension, and when in November 1550 the authorities voted to retain, out of the four, only Christmas, he claimed to have had no part in the decision. What in a sense resolved the problem for him was the fact that, in Geneva, Easter, Pentecost and the Sunday nearest Christmas were three of the four Sundays set aside by law for the celebration of the Lord's Supper. These, then, came to represent what we might call the high points in the Reformer's Christian year, and prompted him to preach on their significance.[1]

Given Calvin's reputation as a preacher and the widespread demand for his sermons in printed form, his Christmas, Easter and Pentecost sermons inevitably attracted the interest of publishers. Accordingly, in July 1558, an edition of selected sermons was issued by Genevan printer Conrad Badius, under the title *Plusieurs sermons de Iehan Calvin touchant la divinité, humanité et nativité de nostre Seigneur Iesus Christ. Item, touchant sa passion, mort, resurrection, ascension et dernier advenement. Puis touchant la descente du S. Esprit sur les apostres, et la premiere predication de S. Pierre.* The book consisted of a lengthy exegetical piece (*congrégation)* on John 1:1-5 and twenty-six sermons, seven of which were on the Servant Songs of Isaiah 52–53. The remaining nineteen comprised one sermon on the nativity (Luke 2:1-14), nine on Christ's passion, death and resurrection (Matt. 26–28), four on the ascension (Acts 1:1-11), four on the descent of the Holy Spirit (Acts 2:1-4, 13-24) and one on the last advent (2 Thess. 1:6-10).[2]

[1] On Calvin and the liturgical year, see the discussion by Willem Balke and Wilhelmus H. Th. Moehn, in their introduction to Calvin, *Sermons sur les Actes des Apôtres* (Neukirchen-Vluyn: Neukirchener Verlag, 1994 = *Supplementa calviniana*, VIII), pp. ix-xi.

[2] The sermons were recorded by Calvin's regular stenographer, Denis Raguenier. See, for

The sermons on Isaiah, the single sermon on 2 Thessalonians, the four sermons on Acts 1 and three of the four on Acts 2 belong to Calvin's regular pulpit series. Health and other commitments permitting, the Reformer's custom, as we know, was to preach twice on Sundays and daily on weekdays in alternate weeks. While none of the sermons is dated, the Acts series can be assigned to 1549, and the nativity and passion sermons to 1557–1558. It is possible, moreover, to place them in a narrower temporal framework. Internal evidence shows that, of the sermons on Matt. 26-28, the first two were Sunday sermons, the last sermon, on the resurrection, is explicitly said to have been preached on Easter Day, coincident with the celebration of the Lord's Supper. The remaining six were thus distributed over the daily services of the intervening week (Monday to Saturday), as required by the ordinance of 1544.

The translation offered here is of the nine sermons on Matt. 26-28, the centrepiece, as it were, of the whole collection. Two earlier English translations of the *Plusieurs sermons* exist, the first done by Thomas Stocker in 1581,[1] the second, after a very long interval, by Leroy Nixon in 1950.[2] The reader, it is hoped, will concede that sufficient time has elapsed to justify the appearance of a third, independent, translation.

* * *

Calvin begins his Easter series with Jesus' vigil in the Garden of Gethsemane (Matt. 26:36-46), and having traced the sequence

further details, Rodolphe Peter and Jean-François Gilmont, *Bibliotheca calviniana*, 3 vols. (Geneva: Droz, 1991-2000), II, pp. 676-81.

[1] *Divers Sermons of Master Iohn Calvin concerning the Divinitie, Humanitie and Nativitie of our Lorde Iesus Christe: as also touching his Passion, Death, Resurrection, Ascention, together with the comming downe of the Holy Ghost upon his Apostles* (London: Thomas Dawson for George Bishop, 1581).

[2] *The Deity of Christ and other Sermons* (Grand Rapids, MI: Wm. B. Eerdmans, 1950); reprinted, unrevised and with a new title, *Sermons on the Saving Work of Christ* (Pelham, AL: Solid Ground Christian Books, 2011).

of events to his death on Calvary (Matt. 26:47–27:66), he concludes with the account of the resurrection (Matt. 28:1-10). The preacher does not, however, confine himself to Matthew's text, but supplements it with material from the other Evangelists, and notably from John, whom he closely follows in his exposition of Jesus' trial before Pilate (John 18:36-19:11), his last moments on the cross (John 19:23-37) and his burial (John 19: 38-42).

It is not easy to preach on the events of that first Easter week. A bare narrative will not do, yet what is told is absolutely unique, and the conflict portrayed so searing that a rare degree of sensitivity, humility and awe is required if the preacher is to do justice to his text. He is standing, in a real sense, on holy ground. How, after all, can the inexpressible be expressed and mystery fathomed, given that it was the Creator who was mocked by his creatures, the Lord of glory who was crucified, and the sinless Son who was condemned in the place of sinners? Nor is there less mystery in the events of the resurrection. The risen Christ is no Enoch of whom it can be said, 'he was not, for God took him' (Gen. 5:24). For a time he continues to walk among men: he speaks, eats, prays, is seen and can be touched, but his body is no longer like ours, and he leaves us with the seemingly paradoxical promise to be absent yet present 'to the end of the world'.

Calvin's detailed exposition is determined by one overarching principle: nothing which happens in this, the climax of the gospel story, is the result of chance or accident. Every event, from the least to the greatest, unfolds according to the sovereign will of God. To call Christ's condemnation a miscarriage of justice is true but scarcely relevant, since it attributes the verdict to the triumph of a determined prosecution over a powerless defence. In Calvin's mind, the key to understanding is furnished not by reference to the operations of an earthly tribunal, but by the word of divine prophecy: 'It pleased the Lord to bruise him' (Isa. 53:10).

Was there no other way? The preacher briefly entertains the question in his opening sermon before dismissing it. He is not interested in speculative solutions to the problem of sin and of man's estrangement from the God who made him. Scripture is the record of what God has done, not of what he might have done. The ultimate answer is known to God alone; it is hidden in his secret counsel, to which not even the angels have access. We must be content – better than content, grateful! – that Scripture tells us all we need to know for our happiness and salvation.

God's sovereignty is nevertheless exercised in such a way that the transgressors – Judas, the priests, scribes and Pharisees, Pilate, the Roman soldiers, the crowd baying for blood – retain full responsibility for their actions. In bondage to Satan, who by God's leave contrives to do his worst, men are his willing agents, his accomplices, his ministers. Like Adam their father they sin knowingly against the light. The evil they do is theirs, not God's, although God is able in his providence to make their evil serve his purposes for good.

Visual representations of Christ's suffering and death, and the meditative exercises associated with them, were a staple ingredient of traditional piety, then as now. To most of Calvin's adult hearers the ritual of the Mass, the Stations of the Cross, the annual feast and eucharistic procession of Corpus Christi and multiple images of the crucified Saviour would have been thoroughly familiar. While omitting none of the details of Matthew's narrative, the Reformer says no more than needs to be said about Christ's vigil in Gethsemane, his trial before Caiaphas and Pilate, his scourging and humiliation on the long road to Golgotha. His attention throughout is directed less to what the eye sees than to Christ's inner agony. What did it cost God's Son to bear the sins of the world and thus to forfeit the Father's fellowship? This is the question he raises in his opening address and which he does not cease to pose in each succeeding sermon. That Jesus feels his solitude in Gethsemane is of course true. That, as man, he shrinks from the suffering to come, is no less true. But neither idea does justice to the dire distress he feels, and which finds expression in the prayer, 'Father, if it be possible …'. Similarly on the cross, the plaintive question, 'Why have you forsaken me?', speaks less of physical pain than of the curse pronounced on sins and thus visited on the sin-bearer. Calvin's belief is that what the Gospel text describes is no less than what the Creed means by Christ's 'descent into hell'. Gethsemane was the first step on that downward path; the cry of dereliction from the cross was the last. 'Not only was his body offered up as the price for our redemption,' writes Calvin, 'but he paid a greater and more excellent price, in suffering the awful torments felt by the lost and the condemned.'[1]

Although the preacher's focus is always on the Christ who endured the cross and who despised its shame, he does not forget the other protagonists in Matthew's narrative. He is alive to the bitterness of Peter's betrayal in the courtyard of Caiaphas' house, a bitterness made all the more poignant by the fact that it is recorded in all four Gospels, and that it is to Peter himself that we owe knowledge of the event. The preacher understands the catastrophe which overtakes Judas, the callous indifference of his priestly allies and the unutterable despair which drives him to suicide. And when the dying thief appeals to Jesus, 'Lord, remember me', how much greater does this miracle of grace appear when, with Calvin, we recall the circumstances in which that plea was made! 'Consider his plight. He is close to death, and suffers awful torment as he waits for someone to come and break his legs and dismember him – torture so bitter and terrifying as to make him lose both mind and memory. He sees our Lord Jesus Christ hanging there, like him, and suffering the greater disgrace. Yet what does he say? He not only acknowledges his faults humbly before God,

[1] *Inst.* II.16.10.

not only assumes the role of teacher so as to bring his companion back to the right path, but makes a confession which, when we look at the facts closely, deserves to surpass all others.'[1]

Basic as the facts of Christ's passion and death are to an understanding of the gospel, to ask 'What?' without also asking 'Why?' is, in Calvin's view, to miss the essentials. It is to come cold to the gospel and to leave it scarcely any warmer. It is no surprise to find that in explaining the significance of the cross, Calvin does not go beyond biblical categories of thought. Why did Christ die? He died, says the preacher, to show the gravity of man's sin and God's abhorrence of it. He gave his life as a ransom, to deliver transgressors from the guilt and power of sin and to relieve them of the curse which the law pronounced upon them. His blood was shed as a sacrificial offering, perfect and complete, to atone for sin, and by washing of the Holy Spirit to sanctify the sinner. He died in our stead, the just for the unjust, that we might be counted righteous in God's sight and fully reconciled to him. He died to demonstrate God's love and pity for the lost, and to destroy the works of the devil.

The preacher's task is not, however, done, once he has answered the questions 'What?' and 'Why?'. It remains for him to press the message home, to demonstrate that doctrine is good only as it engages heart and will, moving us to confess the debt of gratitude we owe to God and our desire to please him. Thus Calvin is at pains to stress what he calls 'the fruit and power of Christ's death' – its efficacy. What then, in practical terms, is the import of the Easter message for the life of faith? How do we benefit from Christ's passion and death? How, to use one of Calvin's favourite metaphors, do we show that we have been profitable scholars in God's school?

We show it by coming to God in repentance, freely confessing our sins and claiming no merit of our own, but seeking to

[1] Sermon 6.

be purged of a guilty conscience and to be forgiven for Christ's sake. We show it by coming in thankfulness to the Father who by grace has saved us, and from whose love nothing can separate us. We show it by coming to him in our weakness, asking to be strengthened by his Holy Spirit so that we may resist temptation, mortify the sin within us and suffer affliction patiently. We show it when we come to him in prayer, relying totally on the Son who knows our nature through and through and who, as our Mediator and Advocate, pleads for us. We show it as we gather in worship to hear the word which feeds our souls, and to share in the sacraments which seal God's promises to us and which witness to our fellowship with Jesus Christ.

There is no less fruit and power in the resurrection than in the cross. Both belong to God's redemptive plan. 'It is not,' says Calvin, 'that Jesus Christ did not cleanse us from defilement by his death and passion, but he could not be left in such a state of weakness. He had to display the power of his Holy Spirit and to show by rising that he was the Son of God.'[1] He who was crucified for our sins was raised for our justification. Because Christ lives, those who through the Spirit are united to him by faith will live also, having already passed from death to life. Moreover the risen Saviour counts us as brethren, and since we are brethren we are, in him, children of God. 'For although he was God's own Son, and although we are only children by adoption and by grace, this commonality remains, namely that he who is Father of our Lord Jesus Christ is, at the same time and through him, our Father.'[2] And since Christ our Head is in heaven, that too is where our life is, hidden with him in God. We live in the light of eternity, anticipating the glory which is to come.

The present translation has been made from the text prepared by the nineteenth-century editors of Calvin's collected works, G.

[1] Sermon 9.
[2] Sermon 9.

Baum, E. Cunitz and E. Reuss.[1] Careful comparison has, however, been made with the original Badius edition held by the Bibliothèque de Genève. Punctuation has been modernized and paragraph divisions introduced. Scripture references have been moved from the margins to the body of the text; they have on occasion been corrected and further references supplied. Sermon headings are my own. The extempore prayers with which Calvin concluded his sermons and which the *CO* editors omitted, have been reinstated. The preacher frequently cites Bible texts from memory; they are translated in the form in which they appear. Some explanatory notes have also been provided.

Annexed to these sermons is a sermon on the ascension (Acts 1:9-11).[2] It is among the earliest of Calvin's sermons whose text has been preserved; it allows another Evangelist, Luke, to continue and, in a sense, to conclude Matthew's narrative of Christ's passion, death and resurrection. 'By his ascension,' says Calvin, 'he has made for us an opening which had been closed through Adam. For since he entered heaven in our flesh and, as it were, in our name, it follows, as the apostle says, that we are now in a sense seated with him in the heavenly places (Eph. 2:6). Ours is no bare hope: we already possess it in our Head.'[3]

I am most grateful to the trustees of The Banner of Truth for their willingness to publish, and express my special thanks to Jonathan Watson, the Editorial Director, for his generous help and guidance.

ROBERT WHITE

Sydney, November 2019

[1] *Calvini opera quae supersunt omnia,* 59 vols. (Brunswick and Berlin: C.A. Schwetschke & Son, 1863–1900), 46: 829-954. (Hereafter cited as *CO.*) The most recent edition of *Plusieurs sermons* is that of Wilhelmus H. Th. Moehn, published in Series V of *I. Calvini opera omnia denuo recognita*, Vol. 8 (Geneva: Droz, 2011).

[2] It is one of four sermons on Acts 1:1-11 which are included in the *Plusieurs sermons* collection (*CO* 48: 577-622).

[3] *Inst.* II.16.16.

I

NO SORROW LIKE HIS SORROW

Then Jesus went with them to a place called Gethsemane, and he said to his disciples, 'Sit here while I go yonder and pray.' [37] *And taking with him Peter and the two sons of Zebedee, he began to grieve and to be sorrowful.* [38] *Then he said to them, 'My soul is sad, even to death. Remain here and watch with me.'* [39] *And going a little further on he fell on his face to the ground, and prayed, saying, 'My Father, if it be possible, let this cup pass from me. Nevertheless not as I will, but as you will.'* [40] *And he came to the disciples and found them sleeping, and said to Peter, 'Could you not watch with me one hour?'*

(Matthew 26:36-40)

When it is a question of our salvation, Scripture sets three objectives before us. The first is that we should know the inestimable love that God has for us, so that we may glorify him as he deserves. Next, that we should come to hate our sins, as is only proper, and should rightly feel such shame that we humble ourselves before the majesty of our God. Third, that we should place such value on our salvation that we are led to forsake this world and all that belongs to this fleeting life, and are drawn instead to that inheritance which has been so dearly won for us. It is to this that we should turn our eyes and apply our minds when we are told how the Son of God redeemed us from everlasting death and obtained for us the heavenly life.

We must learn, then, in the first place, to give God the praise which is his due. He might in fact have snatched us from the pit of death in a different way: nevertheless he chose to display the infinite treasures of his goodness by not sparing his only-begotten Son. Accordingly the Lord Jesus wished to give us an exceptional pledge of his concern for us in willingly surrendering himself to death. For we will never be touched to the quick nor aroused enough to praise our God, unless we examine our condition and are cast, so to speak, into the depths of hell, conscious of what it means to have provoked God's wrath, to have him as our deadly enemy, and as so terrible and awful a judge that it would be much better for heaven, earth and all creation to conspire against us, than to approach God's majesty while it was irrevocably against us. Sinners, therefore, must be stung with an understanding and awareness of their faults, and must recognize that they are worse than wretched. They must feel horror at their plight if they are to know how indebted and bound to God they are for the compassion he shows them, since he sees their hopelessness, and since he resolved to help them even though he saw no merit in them. He thought only of their misery.

Furthermore, because, as I earlier suggested, we are much too wrapped up in the things of earth, and because, when God calls us, our wants and cravings hold us back, we can only properly appreciate the life of heaven if we know at what cost it was won for us. That is why we are told here that not only did our Lord Jesus Christ choose to suffer death and offered himself as a sacrifice to appease the wrath of God his Father, but he stood true and complete surety for us when he did not shrink from facing the anguish awaiting those whose conscience reproves them, and who know that they are guilty, before God, of everlasting death and condemnation.

Observe, then, that God's Son was not content to offer up his flesh and blood and to yield to death; he was also willing to appear before the judgment seat of God his Father for the sake of all sinners and as their representative, ready there to suffer condemnation since it was our burden that he bore. Nor should we feel embarrassed that he subjected himself to such infirmity, for Paul rightly uses his example to urge us not to be ashamed of the preaching of the cross, however foolish it is to some and however offensive to many (1 Cor. 1:23; 2 Tim. 1:8). The lower our Lord Jesus Christ stooped, the more we see that the sins for which we were accountable to God could not be blotted out until he had gone to the bitter end. We know indeed that he became weak so that we might be strengthened by his power, and that he chose to share all our sufferings, except for sin, so that today he might be quick to help us (Heb. 4:15). For if he had not, in his own person, felt the fears, doubts and torments which we endure, he would not be ready, as he now is, to show us pity.

We say that anyone who does not know what hunger or thirst is will never be moved by pity or kindness toward those who suffer, because he has always lived a life of ease and pleasure. Now it is true that although God in his nature does not experience feelings as we do, he does not fail to show us kindness. This is because he is the fount of all goodness and mercy. However, so that we might have assurance that our Lord Jesus knows our weaknesses and can help us bear them, and so that we might come all the more boldly to him and by a more direct route, the apostle declares that he was tempted just as we are (Heb. 2:18). So when the text which we have read says that our Lord Jesus *came to a place called Gethsemane*, and later to the Mount of Olives, we must understand that it was to offer himself as a willing sacrifice, and to show that he meant to fulfil the duty and responsibility entrusted to him. For why did he take our flesh and nature upon himself if not to make up for our rebelliousness by his obedience, so that we might obtain full and perfect righteousness before God his Father?

Thus he offered himself up to death because we could not be reconciled by any other means, nor could we appease God's wrath which our sin had provoked except by his obedience alone. That is why God's Son came freely to the place where he knew Judas was to find him. Know, then, that since our father Adam had brought destruction on us by his rebellion, it was necessary for God's Son, who reigns supreme over every creature, to submit, taking the role of a slave. Hence he is called the servant both of God and of all his people (Isa. 42:1). In the same way Paul, in order to show how reliant we must be on God when we call upon him, fully trusting him to answer the prayers of us, his children, declares that through the obedience of our Lord Jesus Christ we are counted righteous (Rom. 5:19). It is like a cloak which serves to cover all our sins and transgressions, so that God takes no account of what might hinder us from obtaining grace.

On the other hand we see that our redemption came at a very high price: our Lord Jesus Christ experiences such deep distress and suffers the terrors of death – to the point indeed that he sweats drops of blood. He is, so to speak, quite carried away, asking that, if it be possible, he might escape such anguish. To see these things ought to make us conscious of our sins. There is no place here for dreamy self-indulgence when we see the Son of God so utterly overwhelmed that he seems to be in the deepest of pits. If this had happened to a righteous man we should certainly feel moved since, in order to ransom us, he would have suffered what befell the Son of God. Yet here we have one who is the source of life surrendering himself to death! He who upholds the world by his power is made weak! He who keeps all creatures safe from fear has himself to endure such terror! When, therefore, these things are made known to us, we would have to be more than senseless if we did not look within and, being reproved for our faults and iniquities, did not feel shame before God, sighing and groaning, especially if, as a result, we were not led to God with true repentance. Men cannot rightly turn to God unless in themselves they stand condemned, and feel both fear and anguish at the prospect of the curse prepared for them if they are not restored to God's grace.

To give us a better understanding of all these things, we are told that our Lord Jesus *took only three of his disciples*, leaving the rest of the company far off. Even so he does not take the three with him, but prays to God his Father in secret. So we notice that our Lord Jesus has no companion with him when he offers himself as a sacrifice for us. He alone accomplished and fulfilled all that was necessary for our salvation. This is made even clearer to us when we read that *the disciples fell asleep*. They could not be woken up, although they had been warned many times that the hour was coming in which our Lord Jesus was to suffer for the redemption of the human race, and although for three or four hours he had not stopped exhorting them and telling them of his approaching death. In the face of all this they nevertheless fell asleep. Here we see, as in a real-life portrait, that the Son of God had to bear our burdens by himself: no help could be expected from anyone else.

This was meant to give us food for thought, so that we did not speculate wildly as poor unbelievers do who cannot be content with our Lord Jesus Christ, but who imagine that they need protectors and advocates, as if there were any number of redeemers. So we see the cursed blasphemies which prevail in popery, where meritorious deeds serve to enhance the death and passion of our Lord Jesus Christ, and which thus allow us to go free, relieved of the debt we owe to God. Although they insist that a general remission was obtained from the guilt of original sin, and also from the sins we presently commit, nevertheless all of necessity remains confused. The blood of Jesus Christ is not enough, unless the merits of the martyrs are further added. To these, they say, we must also look for refuge, if God is to be favourable to us.[1]

Seeing that the devil has gone to such extremes, we ought to cling all the more to our Lord Jesus Christ, knowing that only in him is perfect salvation to be found. Accordingly the prophet Isaiah says that God wondered when he saw that there was no one else to help (Isa. 63:5). Admittedly God well knew that he himself must accomplish our salvation, but this was so that we should feel ashamed and not be deceived by our hypocrisy, proving that we had contributed nothing to the forgiveness of our sins, so that he might receive us in his grace and love. We were not meant to run this way or that in order to find mediators for ourselves. To settle the point, then, Scripture says that God looked to his own arm for help, and accomplished everything by his own righteousness, finding no one to be his partner.

This is demonstrated visibly to us when we read that three of the disciples, the cream of them all, fell asleep like miserable beasts. There was only brutish mindlessness in them, which was, we might say, monstrous and unnatural, given that they went to sleep at so critical a time. To help us turn our trust away from every creature and place it wholly in our Lord Jesus Christ, it is said that he himself went forth to the fight.

For the rest, in looking to God his Father, he clearly shows us the remedy we need to relieve our distress, to temper our sadness

[1] The Roman Catholic Church held that baptism effaced the guilt of original sin and of sins committed prior to baptism. Sins committed after baptism could be remitted through contrition, confession, the sacrament of penance and priestly absolution. The notion of a treasury of merits, stored up by Christ, Mary and the saints, both living and dead, on which the penitent might draw, received papal sanction in 1343. The invocation of the saints was a practice which the church had long observed, and was reaffirmed as 'good and beneficial' by the Council of Trent in its final session of 1563.

and even to rise above it when we feel depressed. For if we are grieving and in distress, we know that God is not called 'the father of all comfort' in vain (2 Cor. 1:3). If we are separated from him, where else will we find strength if not in him? So we see that, in time of need, God's Son did not hold back. He therefore leads us by his example to our true refuge whenever we are sad and in distress.

Observe, however, the form he uses when he prays: *'My Father, if it be possible, let this cup be taken from me'* – or, instead of 'cup', 'drink', for in speaking of a goblet, cup or glass, he is using a metaphor. Scripture thus calls afflictions 'bitter drink', so that we might know that nothing happens by chance, but that God, like any good family head, apportions to each as he pleases. As, then, a father will give to each of his children his share, or a master to each of his servants, so God shows that it is by him and his hand that they are beaten and afflicted. So too, when good befalls us, it comes from his unmerited kindness, and he gives as much of it to us as he chooses. According, therefore, to this natural way of speaking, our Lord Jesus describes his death as a drink so bitter that he wishes it were taken from him – 'if it were possible'.

Of course we might raise many questions here, for at first glance Jesus Christ would seem to have forgotten our salvation, or else by shunning battle to have given us up as lost because of the fear he felt. That, however, would be at odds with what we said before: it would greatly obscure the love he showed us. We do not need to enter into such involved arguments, since we know that very often intense feeling so grips a man's mind that he ceases to think of one thing or another. Hard pressed by the affliction of the moment, he breaks out, dismissing all thoughts of moderation from his head. When, therefore, we find ourselves quite overwhelmed, it does not mean that everything else is banished from our hearts and that we cease to be concerned.

Someone, for example, who is thinking of some trouble in the church – some very specific trouble – will pray to God as though he cared nothing for the rest of the world. Does this mean that he has lost all kindliness, and is indifferent to his brethren who also need prayer on their behalf? Not at all! The fact is that his concern so powerfully impels him that all else is, as it were, set aside for a time. Moses asks to be blotted out of the book of life (Exod. 32:32). If we wanted to examine every detail of the story, we might say that Moses blasphemed against God by suggesting that God might change his mind, for those whom God has chosen for eternal life can never perish. Moses thus seems to be fighting against God, and trying to make out that God is just like us who change our purposes and plans. How can Moses be said to honour God when, knowing that God had marked him out from childhood and given him the splendid task of leading his people, he nevertheless asks God to end his life and wipe him out? What should we say to that? We could, then, argue at length, but there is a simple solution. Moses was so zealous and passionate for his people that, learning of the terrible threats which God's lips had uttered, he briefly forgets himself and thinks only of what will help his people.

This is how it was with our Lord Jesus Christ. If he had had to endure a hundred – no, a million! – deaths, he would most certainly have prepared himself beforehand. Even so he chose, not so much for his sake as for ours, to suffer the anguish which, as we see, closes in upon him. That is one point.

A second point is this. We may wonder how Jesus Christ, who is absolutely just, the Lamb without spot, the standard and mirror of all righteousness, holiness and perfection, should have willed something different from God's will. The answer is that while God has in himself the very fullness of righteousness, the angels, although conforming to God's will and wholly obedient to it, have a will distinct from his. Inasmuch as they are created beings, they may have feelings which do not belong to God. As for us, who are beset by this mass of sin, we are so confused that we are a long way from God's will. There is something excessive in all our passions, and often indeed there is open rebellion. Even if we think of man in his integrity, that is, uncorrupted by sin, it is certain that he would have had wishes which were very far from God, yet which were not on that account bad or wrong. Supposing Adam had not become corrupt and had continued in the state in which he had been created, he would nevertheless have felt heat and cold, and would have suffered worry, fear and so on. It was the same with our Lord Jesus Christ. We learn that in everything he felt there was neither spot nor stain, all being patterned on obedience to God. Nevertheless, since he had taken our nature on himself, he was inevitably subject both to fear and to the terror we are talking about; subject too to worry and to things of that kind.[1]

This may not be clear to us, since in muddied water we cannot make anything out! Our human feelings toss us this way and that on a sea of emotions; with the result that we need God to steady us. Our passions are like a quagmire which reeks of every infection imaginable, so that we cannot contemplate the kind of suffering felt by our Lord Jesus Christ, if we judge it by our own experience. Even supposing our purposes were good and our

[1] In expounding Christ's prayer in Matt. 26:39, Calvin seeks in part to answer unnamed critics who accuse him of attributing unworthy motives to the Saviour. He therefore argues (1) that we cannot judge Christ's state of mind by our own, chaotic, emotional experiences; (2) that Christ, as man and as our unique sin-bearer, experienced real anguish in Gethsemane, but anguish consonant with faith. Cf. *Inst.* II.16.12: 'These detractors ... do not recognize that such weakness in Jesus Christ was innocent of every fault and blemish, since it was held within the bounds of obedience to God. Because we cannot perceive any proper moderation in our own corrupt nature, and because all our passions are, by their impulsiveness, troubled and excessive, they measure the Son of God by the common standard. There is, however, a great difference, for he, being blameless and without any stain of imperfection, had feelings so well tempered that no excess was to be found in him.'

wishes upright and approved by God, we would still fall short. For example, is it not a good and holy thing for a father to love his children? Yet even here we sin, for the balance and moderation required are lacking. There are faults in whatever virtues we possess. God makes us conscious of them, the better to cast down all pride, to give us cause to hang our heads and to be overcome by shame, since even the good is corrupted by indwelling sin, of which we are chock-full.

As for our Lord Jesus Christ, we must not, I repeat, be surprised if, as man, he wished for something different from the will of God his Father. We must not, however, consider him to be at fault or guilty of transgression. In fact, as we said earlier, we see in these things the inestimable love he bore us, when, faced with such a dreadful death, he willingly yielded to it. But supposing he felt no repugnance, and without a word of protest sipped the cup and found no bitterness in it, what would it mean to have redeemed us like that? It would have seemed merely a game! The fact, however, that our Lord Jesus Christ suffered such distress shows that he so loved us that he forgot himself, allowing the entire storm to break over his head and so free us from God's wrath.

It remains for us to note that the Son of God did not endure all this anguish simply because he had to leave this world. For if that meant only the parting of the body from the soul and the experience of bodily pain, it would not have distressed him so. We must rather notice the quality of his death and consider what lies at its heart. For death does not only dissolve man but makes him feel the curse of God. Not only does God remove us from this world, not only are we lost to this present life, death ushers us as it were into the pit of hell. Where death is concerned we must be estranged from God and cut off from all hope of salvation – unless, that is, we have this remedy: our Lord Jesus Christ suffered for us, so that the wound in us should not prove fatal. For without him we were pierced by death, having no longer any hope of salvation. Now, however, death's sharp point is broken, and its poison so purged that though death brings us low, it now serves as medicine. It is no longer fatal, because Jesus Christ has swallowed all the evil that it contained.

This, then, is what we must remember when God's Son cries: 'Father, if it be possible, let this cup be taken from me.' He had in view not merely the sufferings he was to endure in his body, or the calumnies of men, or his departure from the earth. That would have been easy for him. Rather he sees himself before God and before God's judgment seat, called to account for all our sins, and God's curse already prepared.

Even if there were but one sinner, what would God's wrath be like? But when we learn that God is against us, and wills to put forth his power to destroy us, alas, what can we do? Now Jesus Christ had not only to battle against such fears, but against all the brutality which men might muster. So when God summons before him all who merit everlasting condemnation and who are guilty of sin, and when we see him ready to pronounce the sentence they deserve, who will not at once imagine all the deaths, fears and terrors that each may feel? What a chasm lies before him! Now it was necessary for our Lord Jesus Christ, for him alone and with no other aid, to bear this burden. Let us judge, then, the sorrow of God's Son by its real cause.

Now let us return to our earlier point, which is that we should first know how dearly our salvation cost him, and how precious our souls were to him when he chose to go to the utmost end for our sake. Let us acknowledge also what it was that we deserved; let us think of what our plight would have been if he had not come to our aid. Let us therefore rejoice, seeing that death has no longer any power to harm us. True, we will have a natural fear of death and will shun it, but this is to remind us of the priceless blessing obtained for us by the death of God's Son. It also serves to help us recall what death is in itself, being as it were the pit of hell, expressive of God's wrath.

Moreover, since we have to struggle with such dread, we need to know that our Lord Jesus Christ made provision for all our fears, and that even in the midst of death we can still come before God with our heads held high. Of course we must above all humble ourselves, as we said before. If we are to hate our sins and to have no liking for them we must be moved by God's judgment and terrified by the thought of it. Nevertheless we must lift our heads when God calls us to him. This also is how believers receive encouragement, since Paul writes that Jesus Christ has a crown prepared for all who await his coming (2 Tim. 4:8).

If, then, we have no hope of life when we come before the heavenly Judge, we are sure to be rejected by him. He will not acknowledge us but will disown us, even though we make profession of the Christian faith. We can only await the coming of our Lord Jesus Christ if we are persuaded and convinced that he so battled with the terrors of death as to free us from them and to win for us the victory. And although we will always struggle to be conscious of our weaknesses, to turn to God for help and to be continually made to confess our sins so that God alone is seen to be righteous, we can nevertheless be sure that Jesus Christ has fought for us and gained the victory, not for himself but for us. We cannot doubt that through him we may now surmount all worry, fear and dread, and call upon God, certain that he will always receive us with outstretched arm.

It is important that we remember this. We should be clear that there is nothing speculative about the message that our Lord Jesus suffered the awful terrors of death, and that he deliberately stood surety for us before our Judge, so that, because of the battle he fought, we today may triumph over all our infirmities and may persistently call upon God's name, never doubting that he will answer us and will always be ready in his goodness to receive us to himself. Thus we will pass through life and death, through fire and water, knowing that our Lord Jesus Christ did not fight in vain but gives victory to all who come to him in faith. That, in sum, is what we need to bear in mind.

It is also clear that we must struggle against our own feelings, and that, failing this, it is impossible for us to move a finger without at the same time provoking God's wrath. For here we see our Lord Jesus Christ who, as we said, is pure and blameless. If we ask what his will was, it was admittedly weak, like any human will. But he was not at fault, as is the case with those who are corrupt in Adam. There was no spot of sin in him. Here, then, is a man innocent of any wrong. Nevertheless he must strain every nerve, must struggle and finally deny himself, trampling all else down in order to make himself obedient to God his Father.

Now think of how it might have been with us. What are our feelings like? Our thoughts? Every one of them is the enemy of God; they are at war with him, as Paul says (Rom. 8:7). God, then, declares that we are completely sinful, and that everything we conceive in our heads is vanity and lies. Indeed from childhood on we are steeped in sin's infection. Although when infants come into the world their evil is not apparent, they cannot fail to be small serpents full of poison, malice and contempt. These things, we recognize, are in our nature – yes, from the very beginning. And what are we like once we come of age? We are, as I said, so evil that we cannot frame a single thought which is not in rebellion against God. We can never commit ourselves to one thing or another without straying from the rule of goodness, and without hitting out at God as if we meant to spite him.

What a fight we need to put up, then, in order to obey what is right! When we see that our Lord Jesus, who was entirely innocent and just, could only submit to God his Father by denying himself, we are required to exert ourselves to the full. Let us learn to fight more valiantly. This we cannot do in ourselves: instead all our talents and energies tend toward evil, and we have not one drop of goodness in our nature. We are so feeble that we are defeated every single moment of the day. Since this is so, let us come to him who became weak so that we might be filled with his strength, as Paul says (2 Cor. 12:10, 13:4). Because our Lord Jesus Christ thus denied himself, if we would be his disciples let us learn to do the same. And as we cannot succeed in our own strength, but tend rather to go backwards, let us pray that by the power of his Holy Spirit he may master us and give us strength. As Scripture says, he suffered in the weakness of his flesh, but was raised in the power of his Spirit, so that we should share in the fight he fought, and should feel the fruit and excellence of his power (2 Cor. 13:4; Eph. 1:19). This is what we must remember when we read that Jesus Christ wholly resigned his will in order fully to obey God his Father.

We should always be mindful that here the Son of God not only presents himself as an example and mirror, but desires us to know how high a price he paid for our salvation. For the devil, seeking to veil God's infinite grace displayed in our redemption, insists that Jesus Christ was simply a model of all goodness. This is the way those canting hypocrites in popery twitter on, for although they cannot explain what obedience and denial of self are all about, they hold that what the Evangelist says about Jesus Christ is meant to make us follow his example and to pattern ourselves on him.

Now that is good as far as it goes, but it is not the whole or even the principal thing. An angel could have been sent to us to provide an example for us to follow. Jesus Christ, however, was the Redeemer of the world; he willingly yielded and surrendered himself to the wretched condition in which we see him here. Bear this in mind: we, who can find nothing in ourselves to give us hope of salvation, must look to him for what we lack. We can never obtain God's grace nor draw near to him, unless we come as miserable beggars to Jesus Christ. This is impossible until we acknowledge our poverty and our need – in a word, our utter destitution. Remember this. We have heard that to be perfect we must live in obedience to God, must renounce our thoughts and wants and all that our nature contains if we are to be made like him. We have heard too that we must ask God for what we do not have. Knowing this, let us be assured that our Lord Jesus Christ is not only given to us as an example, but has also shown that, if separated from him, our life can only be accursed. In death we will see the curse as a chasm and God's wrath opening as a pit to swallow us, while we ourselves are gripped with not one fear but a million, as every creature cries vengeance against us.

We should feel this, then, and groan inwardly with shame, wishing with all our heart to come to God with true humility and repentance. We should also pray for God's goodness and pity according as we see them here. May our lips be opened to offer him the sacrifice of praise, and may we turn away from Satan's enticements, for his nets are spread to keep us captive to this world. May we also give up our comforts and our ease, and long instead for the heavenly inheritance which has been so dearly purchased for us. And since next Sunday we are to receive the holy Supper of our Lord, and since God, having opened the kingdom of heaven to us, provides for us a spiritual banquet there, may we be all the more moved by the teaching we have heard.[1]

When we daily eat and drink for our refreshment, God bears ample witness that he is our Father and that he is concerned for

[1] The Lord's Supper was celebrated in Geneva four times yearly: at Easter, Pentecost, the first Sunday in September and the Sunday nearest Christmas day. Prior notice of the sacrament was required to be given, as here.

these earthly and perishable bodies of ours. We cannot eat a piece of bread without having proof of God's care for us. The Supper, however, exists for a special reason. In it God does not fill our bellies but draws us up to the kingdom of heaven. He sets before us the Lord Jesus, his Son, to be our food and drink. And Jesus Christ is not content merely to welcome us to his table; he desires at the same time to be our food. He allows us to experience in actual fact that his flesh is truly food and his blood, drink. Seeing, then, that our Lord Jesus invites us so sweetly to come to him, would we not be utterly vile if we did not withdraw from all that turns us away from him? And although we may come dragging our feet, let us not fail to hate our faults, so that we yield ourselves to him and do all we can to break free of this world and to yearn for the kingdom of heaven.

Consider, therefore, how useful the Lord's Supper can be to each of us. Since our Lord Jesus calls us to share in his death and passion, let us enjoy the fruit he has won for us, and let us be fully assured that God reckons us as his children, and that with full voice we may call upon him as our Father. Let us come with true faith, knowing why our Lord Jesus was sent to us by God his Father, what his office is, and how he is still today the Mediator that he has been from all eternity. And let us seek to be so united to him that what we are told is not for us only as individuals, but is for all in every age. So let there be mutual harmony and brotherhood among us, since Jesus Christ bore the condemnation passed by God his Father upon us all. Let that be our aim, and let each of us not only come for himself but, as I said, let him try to draw his friends in also. May we thus encourage each other to walk steadfastly, always considering our life to be a kind of path which we must tread to the very end. May we not grow weary half-way through, but may we make progress every day and strive to bring closer those who are far off, so that this may be our joy, our life, our boast, our satisfaction. And let us aid and assist each other, until God fully gathers us to himself.

> Now let us cast ourselves down before the majesty of our good God, acknowledging our faults and praying that he may so make us feel them that we may not only cease to like them but may more and more be rid and cleansed of them. May we do battle with ourselves, so that he alone may have mastery over us, and may we heartily consent to do his holy will. May he also be pleased to look with merciful eye upon his poor world , and since he wills that his only Son should be the Redeemer for all in general, and that the gospel should be preached to all, let him not allow men today to harden their hearts and to turn from so good a gift, but may they be attentive, and may we draw each other in, until he brings us to himself in all perfection.

2

TESTED AND BETRAYED

Then Jesus came to his disciples and found them sleeping; and he
said to Peter, 'Could you not have kept watch with me for one hour?
41 *Watch and pray, so that you do not enter into temptation; for the*
spirit is willing but the flesh is weak.' 42 *He went away a second time*
and prayed, saying, 'My Father, if it is not possible for this cup to pass
from me, cause me to drink it. Your will be done.' 43 *Then he came*
and again found them asleep, for their eyes were heavy. 44 *And leav-*
ing them he went away again, and prayed a third time, saying the
same words. 45 *Then he came to his disciples and said to them, 'Sleep*
now and take your rest. Behold the hour is coming when the Son of
man will be delivered into the hands of the wicked. 46 *Rise, let us go.*
See, he who will betray me is approaching.' 47 *And while he was still*
speaking, behold Judas, one of the twelve, came, and with him a large
company with swords and staves, from the chief priests and elders
of the people. 48 *Now he who betrayed him had given them a sign,*
saying, 'The one whom I kiss is the man. Seize him.' 49 *And immedi-*
ately turning to Jesus, he said, 'Greetings, Master,' and he kissed him.
50 *Jesus said to him, 'Friend, why have you come?' Then they came up*
and laid hands on Jesus, and seized him.

(Matthew 26:40-50)[1]

[1] A second set of weekday sermons exists on Matt. 26:40–27:66, dating from March

We saw this morning that the Son of God was obliged to sustain a most difficult fight, having to appear before the judgment seat of God his Father and to accept as our surety the sentence of condemnation. It was inevitable that human weakness should be found in him, but the fact that for the sake of our salvation he became as nothing in no way diminished his divine majesty.

Notice here that he does not pray once only. Thus we see from his example that he urges us not to faint if our prayers are not granted as quickly as we would like. Those who lose heart when God does not answer their first request show that they do not know what prayer is. For to have God as our refuge means that the right rule is to persist in prayer. Accordingly the principal exercise of faith is prayer. Now faith cannot exist without expectation. It is not a matter of God having to oblige us as soon as we open our mouths and make our requests. Often it is necessary for him to hold off and to let us languish, so that we know what it means to call upon him earnestly and without pretence, and so that we show that our faith is truly founded on his word, that it constrains us and gives us patience to endure, until the time is right for us to receive help.

Observe, then, that our Lord Jesus Christ prayed to God his Father not just once: *he returned to prayer a second time.* Remember too that, as was hinted at earlier, he did not merely utter some slight, trivial prayer. It was as if he sought to strip himself bare! Yes, he who is the power of God the Father himself, a power which upholds the entire world, nevertheless, having to appear with the weakness of man, taking our place and representing our very selves, proved that in repeating his prayer it was no mere show he was putting on, as a number of impious people think who believe that when Jesus Christ appeared he did not really

---

1562: *Psalmpredigten, Passions-, Oster- und Pfingstpredigten*, ed. Erwin Mülhaupt (Neukirchen-Vluyn: Neukirchener Verlag, 1981 = *Supplementa calviniana*, VII), pp. 110-69.

suffer.[1] Instead he sought to teach us that only by this means could we escape the hand of God and his curse.

It is clear, then, as we saw this morning, that our Lord Jesus Christ was pressed to the ultimate degree, because the burden he had received was impossible to bear if the invincible power of God's Spirit had not been working in him. We should not think, either, that *when he repeated the same words*, these were superfluous. There is indeed another verse which tells us not to use vain repetitions, as those do who imagine that by droning on they will receive much more (Matt. 6:7). That verse does not, however, mean that we should not continue in prayer: it simply censures the hypocrisy and superstition of those who believe that by assaulting God's ears, so to speak, they can induce and persuade him to grant whatever they want. Such foolishness, we know, has always prevailed among men. Among us, even, are there not many who still go in for this kind of sorcery? Though they may no longer recite the *Ave Maria*, when they say their *Pater noster* they fancy they have gained a great deal, and that God will tot up all the words they have uttered in their prayers! Now I call that sheer sorcery, for they profane the prayer given to us by our Lord Jesus Christ, in which he provides us with a summary of all that we can ask from God and that we may lawfully desire.

Nevertheless none of this prevents someone who is in the grip of distress from turning often to God, and having breathed a few sighs from immediately starting again. When, therefore, we set out to pray, impelled by strength of feeling, not by self-interest or by outward show, nor thinking that we can gain something by prattling on – this is how we show real perseverance, after the example of our Lord Jesus Christ.

[1] Apart from ancient sects such as the Manicheans and Marcionites, who rejected the idea of a physical incarnation, Calvin perhaps has in mind the Spanish savant, Servetus, who denied the full humanity of Christ, or Menno Simons, an influential Dutch Anabaptist, who believed in a Christ 'clothed in celestial flesh'.

The point we should note – one we have mentioned before – is that the main thrust of all our requests is that God should have mastery over us in such a way that we quietly consent to yield to his good will. That, I repeat, is binding on us. So here we have our Lord Jesus Christ: his feelings are just, holy and in accord with righteousness; yet possessing a human nature he has to battle against the sorrow and anguish which have seized him, while holding himself captive in obedience to God his Father.

How, then, is it with us, who are evil and rebellious through and through, and who are so corrupt that we cannot turn our minds to anything at all without offending God? That being so, when we pray to God let us keep so tight a rein on ourselves that none of us takes the liberty, as we usually do, of following our own desires. We can be sure that we have made progress if we can hold ourselves captive and allow God to have dominion over us.

Notice next the words which our Lord Jesus addresses to his disciples: '*Watch and pray, so that you do not enter into temptation, for if the spirit is willing, the flesh is weak.*' Here he shows that the thing which should most spur us to call upon God is that we have a battle to fight. Our enemies are close and they are strong; we could not withstand them unless we had help from on high – unless, that is, God were fighting for us. We know that when someone feels confident, he wants nothing else than to rest in complete comfort and to go to sleep. We become worried or downcast only when need compels us. True, to be at rest is a sovereign blessing, yet only the mindless, we believe, can be at rest. In any case we are only awake when there is some pressing need.

Our Lord Jesus Christ, therefore, had good cause to warn us of the alarms we have to face. What he said to his disciples on this one occasion is relevant to everyone in every age, for in the course of our life we must always be prepared for many trials. If we are members of our Lord Jesus Christ, the devil is our perpetual enemy. There will thus be open, continual and endless war. Think too with what kind of enemy we have to deal: not one adversary, but a countless host! Moreover the devil has any number of means by which he can crush us. At one time he will openly strike at us; at another he will work by underhand means, and he will surprise us by craft a hundred thousand times before we even think of it. Even if all we had was Paul's statement that our enemies are the powers which reign in the air overhead (Eph. 6:12), and that we ourselves are like earthworms crawling about on the ground, that would be cause enough for worry. Peter also makes the same point: our enemy is like a roaring lion in search of prey, and is never at rest (1 Pet. 5:8). This is what we have to remember when our Lord Jesus warns us to be on our guard, lest we enter into temptation.

Moreover, however alert we are and however watchful, we cannot prevent the devil from rising up and attacking us in many different ways. We cannot ward off his blows from so great a distance; but before engaging him in combat, we must be careful not to plunge into temptation. Let us learn, therefore, that although believers and God's children long for rest, they must nevertheless not seek to be comfortable here below. Let it be enough for them that God makes his strength perfect in their weakness, as Paul says when speaking of the path he too had to take (2 Cor. 12:9). It is, I say again, the lot of all of God's children to have to struggle in this world, because they cannot serve God without meeting opposition. Yet however frail they are, however much hindered and struck down, let them be content to be helped and aided by God's hand, and let them rely on the promise that our faith will overcome the world (1 John 5:4).

In any case the remedy is set before us: we must fight on. Satan, it is true, will not fail to renew his attacks on us, but Jesus Christ bids us watch as well.

He further insists that those who presume on their own strength will suffer defeat at Satan's hands a hundred thousand times, without ever achieving victory. What then must we do? We must confess in all humility that we can do nothing, and must go to our God. This is where our real arms are; this is what removes all fear and dread; this is what can make us resolute and give us the assurance that we will continue safe and sound to the end. When we call upon God, it is as Solomon says: 'God's name is an impregnable fortress where the righteous man finds strong and secure refuge' (Prov. 18:10). The same is said by the prophet Joel: though the whole world should be turned upside down, 'whoever calls on the name of the Lord will be saved' (Joel 2:32; Acts 2:21).

These words apply more particularly to the kingdom of our Lord Jesus Christ, so that we should be absolutely sure that even though, in the face of a thousand dangers, our salvation might seem shaky, God nevertheless has us under his protection. We will feel his power always close and always ready to aid us, provided we seek it by our prayers and supplications. That, in brief, is what we need to remember here.

Now in order to reinforce this truth to us, observe that, in his prayer, our Lord Jesus Christ not only called upon God for his own sake and purpose; he consecrated all our prayers and requests so that they are holy, approved by God and pleasing to him. As he says in the seventeenth chapter of John, he sanctifies himself so that we might all be sanctified in him (John 17:19). We must also conclude that he prayed in such a way that his prayer is valid and effective even today, ensuring that God will hear the prayers of all of us.

It is a point greatly to be prized that he goes on to say that *the spirit is willing but the flesh is weak.* He seeks to show us that we all need the remedy which he here prescribes for his disciples. For there are many who think that when they have some worthy feeling, the game is won. This makes them careless, so that they later grow so cold and lazy that they pull back from God and despise his help. For this reason God often withdraws from them and conceals his power, for it is only right that men who are over-confident should suffer disappointment and that God should mock their arrogance and silly fantasies. All, both great and small, should know that they cannot do without God's help, and that whatever gifts they have received, God must always sustain what he has placed in them, increasing his gifts indeed so as to give them added strength.

Thus the spirit is said to be willing but the flesh weak. In other words, although we feel in us some measure of goodwill, although God may have stretched out his hand and already put us on the right path, although we may feel that he truly rules us by his Holy Spirit – although we may feel all of this, we must not be slow to pray. Why? Supposing we were only spirit, we would surely discover much residual weakness in us. And although God may have been at work in us so that we have reason to give him thanks and to exalt his goodness, the fact remains that we would still have cause to hang our heads and to admit that, were he to desert us, we would immediately be – I do not say 'weakened' – but totally ruined.

In a word, our Lord Jesus here tries to show that those who are most mature, who have gone furthest and in whom God has displayed the gifts and power of his Holy Spirit, must nevertheless humble themselves and walk with fear and trembling. They must call upon him hour by hour, knowing that it is not enough for him to have begun if he does not also finish; knowing too that all good things must come from him and that, having given us the will to do good, he must give us the strength to carry it out, since perseverance is the most exceptional and rarest gift there is. This is what our Lord Jesus Christ urges on us.

Now if those whom we may call spiritual, that is, who are passionate in their zeal to serve God, who habitually turn to him and are experienced in prayer and supplication – if, nevertheless, they are so weak that, by not invoking God, they are undone in less than a minute, what shall we say about those who are pitifully burdened and earthbound, so that they cannot drag one leg after another, have one good feeling or one good thought? How hard must these struggle when compared with the others! So let each of us examine himself. We will find that when it comes to prayer we are so dull and sluggish that it is sometimes more a case of ritual performance than of real emotion. That being so, let us learn to hate our failings and our lazy ways. Let us detest this perversion, and as we strive to call upon God let us lift our spirits on high and look for the remedy offered to us here. That, in sum, is the lesson for us here.

We are told that the disciples fell asleep a third time, despite the fact that they had already been deeply embarrassed – added to which, as we saw this morning, our Lord Jesus Christ alone accomplished our salvation, having no one else to accompany him. Here we should see something of our own indolence, for we are certainly no smarter than these three. Yet they were the leading members of the whole group. Marked out by Jesus Christ as the cream of the twelve, they were to proclaim the gospel throughout the world. Nevertheless, having made so good a beginning they now fail badly, as we see. We are therefore taught to turn wholly to the Son of God and to look to him for everything we lack. Let us not lose heart when we see such frailty in ourselves. True, the apostles' example gives us no cause to feel complacent, as many are who say that they too can go to sleep, since Peter, John and James did the same! We should hate our faults, though always remembering that our Lord Jesus Christ is ready to receive us if we come to him. Moreover there is the particular point which I made this morning: all that is of man must fail. We should recognize that our salvation is accomplished by him who was ordained by God to be our Mediator.

Note also that it is when we are closest to our Lord Jesus Christ that we must be most alert. Worldly people and those whom God has abandoned and completely cut off as rotten limbs experience little by way of conflict. The devil has already mastered them, which is why they are able to sleep in peace. When, however, our Lord Jesus Christ graciously calls us to himself and personally draws near to us, Satan also stirs up conflicts for us, seeking to turn us away from obedience to God. When, I say, he sees that we are doing well, it is then that his attacks are heaviest. Let each of us be ready, therefore, knowing what it is to which God calls us and where our duty lies.

When next it is said, *'Sleep, and take your rest; the hour has come'*, our Lord Jesus Christ makes it clear that they would very soon have been taken by surprise if God had not been watching over them. Even so he rebukes them, saying in effect: 'What, is this what you have come to? The devil is doing all he can to damn the human race. I alone must be the one to restore God's kingdom, otherwise every creature must perish. Yet here you are asleep!' Now on that occasion his warning was of little use, given their ingratitude displayed in such mindlessness and lethargy. In time, however, the disciples came to realize that they must ascribe all praise for salvation to God. So today we are taught that, as I said before, the Son of God, alone and unaided, had to be our Redeemer.

At the same time let us learn that God must watch over us even while we sleep. How often might the devil have oppressed us, and what means do we have to resist him, if God had not had pity on us, as he sees us lying there unconscious? Now this should not deceive us into thinking that we can give up prayers and supplications, but we should always remember what the Psalm says: 'He who watches over Israel neither slumbers nor sleeps' (Psa. 121:4). For our part, then, let us be alert, as we have already been urged to do. Even so, we should be clear that however alert we may be, God must still keep careful watch on us, otherwise our enemies would soon have total victory over us.

Following this, Jesus Christ says to his disciples, *'Let us go; see, he who betrays me is approaching.'* The only reason he does not allow them to keep him company is that they should see that he does not spare himself for their sake or for the sake of all mankind. For he came forward to receive every blow and to save us from them, thus fulfilling the word which said that he would not allow any to perish whom the heavenly Father had given and entrusted to him (John 6:39). With these words he indicates that he goes willingly to death, as we explained this morning. In order to be blotted out, our rebelliousness called for his sacrifice of obedience. If he had not voluntarily offered himself up to appease the wrath of God his Father, his death and passion would have been of no benefit to us. To death, then, he goes, showing that as he took our nature on himself in order to redeem us, so in this crucial act he chose not to fail in his duty.

Our narrative tells us that *Judas had given this sign, that the one whom he would kiss was Jesus; he should be seized.* The kiss was a method of greeting. Just as in some nations people embrace and in others they kiss hands, so the Jews are invariably accustomed to kiss each other, as Scripture shows. For the rest, we might think it strange that Judas, having left the company of Jesus Christ some time before – that very night, in fact – should come back and kiss him as if he had just returned from a distant journey. He performs this ritual, however, because he comes as a man filled with fear. That is why, according to the other Evangelist, he says, 'Rabbi, rabbi, peace be to you' (Mark 14:45). He seems truly grieved to find his master under attack, and seeing so large a crowd coming to take him by surprise, he draws near and kisses Jesus Christ, as if to say, 'Master, people are looking for you. Here are your enemies who surround you; they want to get rid of you. You will be cut off from among men if once they lay their hands on you.' So Judas gives signs of pity and compassion. At the same time we read that Jesus Christ reproaches him, saying, *'Friend, why have you come?'* It is as if he said, 'Wretch, you were with me at my table, and in a way you were part of my body when we were united as God's children. I was your Head, but I acknowledged you as one of my members. Yet now you come to betray me – with a kiss, no less!'

Observe that this was the mark which God's Son had to bear, so that Scripture might be proved right, and so that he might be shown to be the Redeemer chosen by God. For all this was prefigured in the person of David, who was as it were a mirror and image of the Son of God. David therefore says that it was not strangers or open enemies who caused him injury and distress; it was the man who ate bread at his table who treacherously lifted up his heel against him, deceiving and falsely betraying him (Psa. 41:9). Or, as we read in another place, it was the companion who went with him into the house of the Lord (Psa. 55:14). It is as if he were speaking not only of human intimacy and friendship, as happens when we share a life together, but of sacred brotherhood, hallowed in God's name.

This is what the Holy Spirit intended us to see. There was nothing which befell the Son of God which had not been earlier attested and prefigured, in order to strengthen our assurance that it was he who, from the very beginning, had been chosen by God, for he bears such unmistakable marks. We also see in the person of Judas proof that God's church will always be subject to many acts of treachery. True, it is already something when we have Satan and his crew as our enemy, along with all the other things of which we spoke. Nevertheless we also have men who are openly at war with God and who wish only to disturb God's church. It is, I say again, already something when we have to fight against such adversaries, but God desires to test our patience even more in this respect, so that there will always be household enemies in our midst who are disloyal and full of treachery. And although this kind of pestilence is hateful, the church will never be cleansed of it. Of course we need to guard against it, and each must try as much as possible to scrape off such filth and infection. Still, even when we have done everything, God wills that there should always be Judases. For since this was prefigured in David and fulfilled in our Lord Jesus Christ, we must, as Paul says, be conformed to him (Rom. 8:29), for he bears, we might say, the coat of arms of God's house, being the firstborn among the faithful. We must therefore share a common lot with him.

What we witness here, in Judas, are the signs of a terrified conscience, for God put in him the spirit of the whirlwind, of frenzy and of mindlessness, as he often says through the prophets. Judas thus shows us the price paid by those who deliberately fight against God. They are so distraught that they lose all sense and reason. Even so in their hypocrisy they always try to hide it, until God forcefully draws them to him and brings them to final condemnation.

At first glance it might seem that two contradictory things are at work here: that a man should charge at God like a wild bull, and yet so forget that it is pointless to spit at the sun that he dares to defy nature; and that he should use underhand tricks to protect himself while knowing that his hypocrisy will get him nowhere. We might say that these two things are not compatible. Nevertheless we see them in Judas. He had had experience of Jesus Christ's heavenly power, had witnessed many miracles and in Christ's name had done some himself.[1] Knowing, then, that our Lord Jesus Christ had supreme dominion over both life and death, he betrays him and tells them to bind him as a precaution, for otherwise he might have immediately escaped. There we have Judas, who is bereft of all sense and reason, acting like a madman. Yet with a kiss and the honeyed words, 'Alas, Master', he still resorts to subterfuge, thinking to get clear by such means. This is how Satan dazzles those who are in his snare.

Let us learn, then, first and foremost, to humble ourselves so that none of us stumbles against this exceedingly hard stone. In other words, let us not wage war on our Lord Jesus Christ. We should beware of giving vent to our devilish rage, of battling against the truth and of skirmishing against our conscience, so that we knowingly provoke God's wrath by seeking to defy him. Let us beware of doing that, nor should we so indulge in our hypocrisy and make-believe that we end up frustrated and deceived. For we know what happened to Judas, as the story goes on to say: he needed no judge to condemn him or anything to force him to recant. He confessed that he had sold and betrayed innocent blood (Matt. 27:4). Still, he did not ask forgiveness for his crime; he went and hanged himself in despair; it was this that killed him (Matt. 27:5; Acts 1:18).

Accordingly we are warned not to give entry to Satan so that he can blind our eyes when we are asleep in our sins; we must not think that in this way we can escape God's hand. Let us be rid of such pretence. For the rest, remember that we are strictly commanded in the second Psalm to kiss the Son of God (Psa. 2:12), in order to do him homage as to our King, the one who has supreme rule over every creature. For the word 'kiss' signifies that we bow low and solemnly confess that we are his. As he says, 'You call me Master, and you do well' (John 13:13). When, however, we

[1] Cf. Mark 3:14-15, 6:12-13 and Acts 1:16-17.

come to him, let us be careful not to call him 'Master' with the tip of our tongue, while all the time we are his enemy. Let us be careful not to bow before him in pretence while really kicking out at him and digging in the spur! That is, let us not out of disloyalty be surly and rebellious, but let us show that we have sought only to maintain ourselves within his church and to offer worship to our God. Let us make sure we heed this message.

Moreover, although our Lord's words to Judas had no initial effect on him, the fact remains that, by virtue of the word he spoke, Judas hanged himself without waiting for another to condemn him. Indeed John records that our Lord Jesus Christ dismayed all who came looking for him, although he spoke but one word to them, saying 'I am he' (John 18:6). See, here is a detachment sent by Pilate, governor of the country; here too are many men assembled by the priests. They come equipped with staves, swords and other blades. Jesus Christ stands alone – in Isaiah's words, like a lamb brought to the slaughter (Isa. 53:7). And what does he say? 'I am he.' All were immediately thrown back, falling to the ground! How can we explain their fall? It was, we know, because he retained his heavenly power whenever he chose, although he was humbled for a time and became as nothing. Had he wished, he could have crushed all his foes whom Satan, being free to act, had driven to a frenzy of cruelty. The same point is made by Luke: 'This is the reign of darkness' (Luke 22:53).

However that be, in saying 'I am he', Jesus Christ put his enemies to shame. What will it be like, then, when he comes in his majesty with all his angels? When he comes to make all who have resisted him his footstool? Or when he comes with terrifying face and with unimaginable wrath, as Paul writes in the first chapter of Second Thessalonians (2 Thess. 1:7, 8)? How then will the wicked, who despise God's majesty and the word of our Lord Jesus Christ, be able to stand before his face? For even on the point of suffering he struck down his enemies, though using nothing in his defence – nothing, not even the defence supplied by God his Father. As he says, *he could ask for a million angels to be sent to him.* Yet he holds off, while demonstrating that with one word he could have destroyed, had he wished, everything that stood against him.

Thus we are taught to fear the word of our Lord Jesus Christ, and although he is not living in visible fashion among us, because the gospel is proclaimed on his authority, and because he says, 'He who hears you, hears me' (Luke 10:16), let us learn to receive with all reverence what is preached to us in his name, and let us obey it. Then we will find that the word which bowled the soldiers over – they and those who came against him – will be our sole foundation and support. For when will our joy be full, except when the Son of God appears, when we see how near he is to us, when he reveals himself as he is, and shows us why God his Father sent him to us?

The word 'I am he' teaches us that when our Lord Jesus Christ shows himself as he now does to his faithful people, he reveals why he calls us to himself, why he came down to us and why he lives in us by the power of his Holy Spirit. Here we find all our repose and blessing. If, however, we choose to be rough and surly, and like many worldly people scorn God's word on which all of our salvation rests, we can be sure that it will be a thunderbolt which hurls us to destruction into the depths of hell. Let us fear, then, yet at the same time may the Lord Jesus open the door to us, and may he say to us, 'Here I am', in tones different from those he used when addressing his sworn enemies. Let us learn to come to him.

We must also learn to bear patiently the treachery we see in today's church. It should nevertheless be odious to us, so that we might prove that we truly cling to the Son of God, for he is our Head. And since we have his truth, let us so live with one another that we are united in genuine peace and brotherhood. This is something we need to remember.

Let this, however, be the main lesson we glean from this passage. The Son of God showed himself to be wholly obedient in every way, in order to make up for our rebelliousness. All who are members of his body, as I have said, must model themselves on his example. Since he who has all dominion and sovereignty humbled himself, it is only right that we should be ready to obey our God in life as in death. Understand, however, that the obedience which our Lord Jesus rendered is of a special kind, because of its fruit and subsequent effect. The apostles, indeed, regarded the death of Jesus Christ as an example. In time of need it gave them strength when they had to fight for their witness to the gospel. At such a time they did not fall asleep, but were alert and quick to follow their calling. They did not fear torture or death but faced up to them when summoned by God to do so, for the glory of his name and the confession of our Lord Jesus Christ.

More than that, however, they chiefly sought to show that it is through the blood shed by our Redeemer that we are washed and cleansed of all our stains; that he fully paid the price for all the debts to which we were bound; and that he has obtained for us perfect righteousness. Think, therefore, how very different the Head is from the members. Let us learn that by nature we are still completely prone to evil, and that although God has given us in part new birth, our flesh continually resists him. Nevertheless, by virtue of the obedience of Jesus Christ we are acceptable to our God, and even if we do not yet do the good we desire, and if we are often beset by evil so that we fall or are much too slothful, let us look to what the Son of God suffered to make atonement for all our offences. Remember that although he fought, he did not protest when our sins were imputed to him, as we explained at length this morning.

Thus our Lord Jesus Christ made satisfaction for everything, and in every way. Today, although we strive to obey God, we find we cannot succeed: we are forever dragging our feet and are always much at fault. Even so we are still acceptable to God; our imperfections will always be blotted out by the obedience of our Lord Jesus Christ, so that God takes no account of them.

For the rest, let each of us exert himself and battle on according to the measure of his faith and the grace he has received, until we come to our heavenly rest. And since we see how great our weaknesses are, knowing that we cannot have one good thought and that when we stumble we cannot get up again unless God reaches out his hand and minute by minute gives us strength, let us make sure we ask him to increase in us, as he has promised, the gifts of his Holy Spirit, and to grant that our Lord Jesus Christ may be our Head and our commander, so that as we follow him we may obtain the victory he has won for us. Its fruit we already feel, but then we will know it in all its fullness.

> Now let us cast ourselves down before the majesty of our good God, acknowledging our faults so that we may rightly humble ourselves before him and be brought to true repentance. With all our might may we endeavour more and more to banish all that is contrary to his righteousness. And since we can never be free of conflict or rid of our enemies, may he be pleased to extend to us the aid he has promised to all who are his. May we experience his help, therefore, so that, continuing to the end, we are able to withstand every trial. And may we also learn to give him the praise for every victory we win, ascribing nothing to ourselves, lest by our arrogance we provoke his wrath. May we always beg him to continue his gifts in us, and may he ever more pursue the work begun and done in us.

3

ARREST AND PROSECUTION

*And behold, one of those who were with Jesus stretched out his hand
and drew his sword, and struck the servant of the high priest and
cut off his ear. 52 Then Jesus said to him, 'Put your sword back into its
place, for all who take the sword will perish by the sword. 53 Do you
think that I cannot now pray to my Father, and that he will send me
more than twelve legions of angels? 54 How then would the Scriptures
be fulfilled, for it must be so?' 55 At that hour Jesus said to the crowds,
'You came out as against a thief, with swords and staves in order to
take me. Every day I sat in the temple teaching, but you did not take
me. 56 All this has been done that the Scriptures of the prophets might
be fulfilled.' 57 Then all who had seized Jesus brought him to Caiaphas
the high priest where the scribes and elders had gathered together.
58 Peter was following him at a distance, as far as the courtyard of the
high priest, and going inside he sat with the servants to see the end.
59 Now the chief priests, elders and the whole council sought testimony
against Jesus, that they might put him to death, but they found none.
60 Many false witnesses came, but they found none who were ade-
quate. At last two came forward 61 and said, 'He said, "I am able to
destroy God's temple, and in three days to build it again."' 62 And the
high priest stood up and said, 'Have you no answer to make? Why do
these men testify against you?' 63 But Jesus was silent. And the high*

priest said to him, 'I adjure you by the living God, tell us if you are
the Christ, the Son of God.' 64 *Jesus said, 'You have said so. But I*
tell you, hereafter you will see the Son of man seated at the right hand
of power, and coming on the clouds of heaven.' 65 *Then the high priest*
tore his robes and said, 'He has spoken blasphemy. What further need
is there of witnesses? You have now heard his blasphemy. 66 *What is*
your opinion?' Answering, they said, 'He is guilty of death.'

(Matthew 26:51-66)

If, relying on first impressions and on our own judgment, we sought to understand the arrest of our Lord Jesus Christ, we would be troubled by the fact that he offered no resistance. To suffer such shame and indignity without doing anything to stop it would seem to be incompatible with his majesty. We would admire instead the zeal shown by Peter, since he exposed himself to death. For there he could see a large crowd of enemies; he was alone, a man untrained in the use of arms. Nevertheless he unsheathes his sword out of love for his Master, preferring to die on the spot rather than allow him to suffer harm. What we see here, however, is that we must come modestly and humbly if we are to learn the ultimate purpose of all that God's Son suffered, and that what we ourselves think is worth nothing. We must ask God to lead and guide us by his word, and must only decide on the basis of what he reveals to us.

The gospel is a stumbling block to many, while others to their condemnation poke fun at it. They are puffed up with pride and make rash judgments. To avoid all error, then, we must return to what our Lord Jesus said earlier: such was the will of God his Father. That is one point.

Then too, in considering something which seems strange to us, we must think about its purpose. So if we bear these two thoughts in mind we will have cause to worship God, and to realize that what seems foolish to men is of wondrous wisdom even to the angels. But to pursue these things further, let us see what we are told here about Peter: unsheathing his sword, *he cuts off the ear of Caiaphas' servant, Malchus.*[1]

We notice here how headstrong men are when they follow their foolish fancies. They are so blinded that they cannot hold back in any way. Yet when they should be obeying God, it is sad to see how dilatory they are; they forget themselves so often that they turn tail and flee! Thus we are much more courageous in following our absurd whims than in doing what God commands and what our calling requires. Peter's example proves this all too clearly. As we will see later, when he had to confess our Lord Jesus Christ and to testify to him, Peter, to his utter loss, blasphemes. Yet here he is happy to die, even though he is not commanded to do so! What prompts him to unsheathe his sword? He does it, we might say, out of defiance, for he had no such instruction from his Master. And when he denied Christ, did he not remember what was said before: 'He who denies me before men, I will deny before God my Father in heaven' (Matt. 10:33)?

It is as I said, his mind is seething, and he is carried away by the mad desire to protect our Lord Jesus Christ as he chooses and in his own way. May his example teach us to walk according as God calls us, and may we not find it hard to do as God commands. Let us not, however, attempt to do anything, not even to lift a little finger, unless God approves and we have evidence that it is he who is guiding us. So much for that point.

Now our Lord Jesus first makes it clear to Peter that he has deeply offended him, because he was not ignorant of the law which says, 'Whoever sheds human blood, his own blood will be shed' (Gen. 9:6). Peter ought certainly to have remembered the lesson that God will not have us use force or violence. Moreover,

[1] Cf. John 18:10, which identifies Peter as the assailant, and Caiaphas' servant as Malchus.

in what school had he been brought up in the space of three or more years? Had not our Lord Jesus trained him as much as possible to be kind and gentle? How could Peter have got the idea that his recklessness would pass muster?

All the more, then, must we give heed to what was said before, that while men may admire our zeal and applaud it, God will nevertheless condemn us if we transgress his word in however small a way. Praise is only deserved if we walk according to what God shows us in his word, for as soon as anyone goes beyond these bounds, his virtues are merely rotten. That is how it is with all our pious works. When we have laboured hard to do everything our brain conceives, God will condemn it all unless we have his word. That is the only truth that he approves and regards as valid.

Returning, however, to the story we are discussing, we should be even more mindful of the second reason cited by our Lord Jesus Christ. We have already referred to it in general terms, but here we have a verse which strictly concerns his death and passion, when he says, *'Do you not think that I could pray now to my Father, and that he would send me more than twelve legions of angels?'* Now in those times a legion usually consisted of four or five thousand men. 'So there,' he says, 'is a heavenly host which I could have, yet I desist. Why then do you seek here to usurp more than God desires or allows?'

It is of course perfectly lawful for us to call upon God, and to pray that he may preserve our life and keep it under his protection, since he holds it precious. Our Lord Jesus, however, declares that he will not do this now and must not do it. How then can Peter resort to violence, contrary to the order which God permits and has established in his word? If a means which in itself is lawful should not be employed, what shall we say of means which God has forbidden and has pronounced punishable? What we witness here is the Son of God submitting to such abuse, and preferring to let himself be bound and trussed up like a common criminal, than to summon up a miracle and thus prove false, or to have God put forth his arm to defend him. From this we should learn how much our salvation meant to him. In any case we ought to notice the point I made before: Jesus Christ refers us to the will and decree of God his Father, otherwise we would think it strange that he chose not to ask for help which he well knew he could have had.

We might perhaps feel that he is tempting God by not making that request. We have the promise that the angels will surround those who fear God (Psa. 34:7), and that they will bear them up lest they strike their foot, or meet with evil on their way (Psa. 91:11, 12). When God has promised us something, he wants us to be stirred up so that we pray. Thus whenever we are in need we should turn to him so that he might use his angels to direct us, for this is the task he has committed to them. This, we know, was what the holy patriarchs and the fathers practised. 'The angel of the Lord who has never failed me,' said Abraham, 'will be with you on your way and will make you prosper' (cf. Gen. 24:7). All the holy fathers acted this way. Why then does Jesus Christ not want angels who, as Luke says, had earlier comforted him (Luke 22:43)? Angels had also served him by relieving his distress (Matt. 4:11). He appears, then, to scorn God's necessary aid, but in reality he is thinking of what he says next: *'How will the Scriptures be fulfilled?'*

He might have said that if we are fearful of something, we can and should pray to God that he may look mercifully on us and grant us to be made strong by every possible means. When, however, we are sure that there is a trial which we must face, and when God's will is known to us, no other request can be made than that he empower us and grant us invincible steadfastness. We should not object or be driven by our feelings, but should go forward with cheerful hearts to wherever he calls us. For example, if our enemies are persecuting us and we do not know what God has in store for us or what the outcome will be, we must pray to him, because our life is precious to him. Since he has taken charge of it, let him demonstrate the fact: let him deliver us. On the other hand, when we are convinced that God means to call us to himself and when no further remedy remains, we must cease arguing and fully resolve to do no more than obey God's unalterable edict. This is the intention of our Lord Jesus here. He prayed constantly throughout his life, and even before his supreme struggle he prayed that God might allow the cup to pass from him if possible. Now, however, his mind is made up, for such is the command of God his Father. Now he sees that he must fulfil the task entrusted to him, making perpetual sacrifice to wipe away the sins of the world. He sees now that this is his calling and that the question has been settled. He therefore refrains from asking God to do the opposite, nor does he seek help from either angels or men. He does not want God to grant him power and to rescue him from death. It is enough that he is steadfast in spirit, and is able of his own free choice to do what must be done. With that he is content.

What we learn here is that God's will should stop us in our tracks and hold us in check, so that when things seem tough and against all reason, what God has ordained means more to us than anything our brain can apprehend. Our whims and fancies must thus be trodden underfoot once we know that God has other plans. It is part of the obedience of faith to think of God as wise and as having authority to do everything he wishes. And if we have contrary views, we should know that they are mere smoke and emptiness. God knows all things: nothing is hidden from him and his will is the measure of all wisdom and righteousness. The fact that we reason to the contrary reflects our ignorance, for as we know, God's wisdom is infinite, while we have scarcely three drops of common sense in us. Men should not be surprised if God does not behave the way they like. Why not? Because we are poor fools. As long as our mind and reason have the upper hand, we are quite senseless. Therefore since we cannot fathom the bottomless depths of God's judgment, let us learn to worship what is hidden from us – worship it, I say, humbly and reverently, confessing that all that God does is entirely right and just, even though we do not understand how it is so. That is one point.

Notice next that because God willed that his Son should be exposed to death, we must not be ashamed of what he suffered, or think that the wicked had a free hand, or that God's Son did not have the means to defend himself. No, everything was the result of God's will and of his changeless decree. That is why our Lord Jesus Christ says in Luke, 'Now is your reign, and the power of darkness' (Luke 22:53). It is as if he said, 'Do not boast about what you are doing, for the devil is your master.' At the same time he reveals that all this is because God has given them leave to act. And although the devil is driving them, neither they nor he could have attempted anything had not God relaxed the reins. That then, in brief, is why, when we speak of the death and passion of Jesus Christ, we should fix our eyes on the will of God and on his eternal counsel. It is made clear that this was God's will, for *thus it was written*.

If our Lord Jesus had not had evidence of what God his Father had already ordained, he might have hesitated. As it was, he is conscious of his duty. God did not send him to earth without at the same time giving him this explicit task. It is true that, as everlasting God, he did not need Scripture to give him instruction. However, as our Redeemer who clothed himself with our nature so that he might have brotherhood with us, he needed to be taught by holy Scripture. Nowhere, as we see, did he refuse instruction; he was grounded in it, since God had made his calling clear to him. He made himself captive to it, as it were, in order not to retreat when required to fulfil the task entrusted to him.

Accordingly, let us learn that because God's will is secret in itself and beyond our understanding, we must turn to holy Scripture. God, indeed, does not fail to follow his determined counsel in those things which we regard as accidental; his counsel, however, is not made plain to us. We will not always have a special revelation so that we can say that God has determined this or that. We must thus remain uncertain. Hence when we succumb to sickness or to some other affliction, we will ask God in prayer to heal or deliver us. Why? Because we do not know what his wishes are. Of course we should not lay down the law to him, but should always add the proviso, 'his will be done'. Nevertheless all our prayers should aim at asking him for what he knows is necessary and useful to us, but also at committing everything to his secret counsel, so that he might do as he chooses. Even so, when Scripture testifies to something which God wills, there is no room, as I have said, for objections.

This is more clearly shown to us in the case of our Lord Jesus Christ. It was not only by the design of wicked men that he was made to suffer cruelly and was treated with such shame and contempt; it was because God had decreed that it should be so. How is this made clear to us? By holy Scripture. Two thousand years before Jesus Christ was born, had not sacrifice been commanded by the law? And before the law was given or written down, had not God already inspired and taught the patriarchs to offer sacrifice? And could the blood of brute beasts obtain the remission of sins? Not at all! It was to show that God would be reconciled by the blood of the Redeemer whom he had ordained. This was clearly revealed and explicit witness borne to it by the Scriptures. We see how the prophets spoke about it, and how pointedly they are quoted. When Isaiah says that he who was to be the Redeemer would be marred and scorned, and like a leper would have no form or beauty in him, that he would be struck and smitten by the hand of God, and would be dreadful to behold – when, finally, his life would be taken from him (Isa. 53:2-4, 10), by whose power was that prophecy made? Is God incapable of resisting Satan and all the wicked? No! What he announced through the lips of Isaiah was what he had preordained. This thought is even more firmly expressed in Daniel (4:34, 35). Since God had revealed that his only Son must be sacrificed for our redemption, we are confirmed in the truth of what I am saying: in the indignities to which men subjected Jesus Christ, we must always discern the sovereign hand of God.

Thus Peter says expressly in the fourth chapter of Acts that Judas, all the Jews, the soldiers and Pilate did only what the counsel and hand of God had determined (Acts 4:27, 28). It is to this that we must look if we do not want to be troubled by our foolish fantasies. God sent his only Son to earth that he might accept the obedience he would offer to him in his death and passion, thus blotting out all our iniquities and offences. Here, then, is the second point I touched on earlier: the fruit which we owe to the suffering of our Lord Jesus Christ. If we did not know why he suffered, we would cease to have any taste for what we are told here. When, however, we learn that he was bound and shackled for our deliverance, and especially when we discern our natural condition – our bondage to sin and death which makes us slaves to Satan, so that where once we were created in God's image we are now totally corrupt, accursed and dragged like helpless beasts into hellish captivity – when, I say, we discern these things, and see the Son of God not refusing to be shackled in order to break the spiritual chains of sin and death which kept us bound to Satan, then we must triumph aloud in his death and passion and in his arrest of which this passage speaks. This is the point we need to remember here.

The Evangelist next records that *our Lord Jesus Christ healed the servant* whom Peter had injured. Not that he deserved it, but the offence had to be corrected. If the wound had been left as it was, it would have dishonoured the gospel message and the redemption won by Jesus Christ. People might have said that he had resisted the governor of the land and all the priests, and had practised brigandage in this out-of-the-way place. That would have obscured the glory of God's Son and discredited the gospel forever. Peter's gesture was the passionate act of Satan, for the devil schemed to bring disgrace on Jesus Christ and on his message. That is where our beautiful acts of piety lead us when we try to serve God any way we choose, and when we think ourselves free to do whatever seems good to us. Our Lord Jesus thus sought to avert this scandal so that no one could denigrate his teaching.

Even so we see just how detestable and thankless were those who were unmoved by this miracle. Here are the soldiers who come to bind Jesus Christ. They witness the power of God's Spirit who is at work in him in so many ways. A little earlier with one word he had sent them staggering back; now he heals a man with a severed ear, yet it means nothing to them. Once the devil bewitches men and dazzles their eyes, neither God's gifts nor all his powers can move them, can stop them acting like madmen or like swine, thrusting their snouts into everything. Whatever God does or says they remain horribly obdurate. That is why we should ask God in prayer to give us wisdom, so that we may benefit from his favours and be drawn to his love. And when he raises his hand to show us that he is our judge, let us also ask him so to move us that we may be driven back to him by fear and in true repentance. That is the lesson for us here.

At any rate, the mouths of the wicked were stopped when our Lord Jesus Christ healed the servant. Following this we read that *Jesus was taken into the house of Caiaphas, and there was questioned.*

For the sake of brevity we will omit what John says concerning Annas, who was Caiaphas' father-in-law (John 18:13-24). Perhaps it was out of respect that Jesus Christ was taken to him, or because that was where the road led until such time as all might assemble together. Jesus is thus brought into Caiaphas' house, where, we read, *the priests sought false witnesses everywhere. At last two got up and said: 'He said that he would rebuild the temple in three days.'*

An accusation is thus brought against our Lord. Not that the priests were really moved by zeal, as those are who persecute the innocent, thinking that they are doing acceptable service to God, or in the manner of Paul who was so infuriated that he sought men out like a brigand (that is how he calls himself), in order to ruin and lay waste everything, for he regarded himself as a zealot (1 Tim. 1:13). It was not the same, however, with Caiaphas and his lackeys. What was it they were out to do, if not to oppress Jesus Christ unjustly? So self-interest led them to do open battle with God, which is a dreadful thing. Yet Caiaphas and his associates were children of Levi, part of the holy line that God had chosen. They had not been chosen by men, for God had decreed through the law that it must be so (Num. 1:48-50). There was in those days, it is true, wicked and foul corruption, because the priesthood could be bought, and instead of being for life as God had commanded, one man might expel a colleague, the title going to the highest bidder. There was corruption, then, foul and detestable, and any number of conspiracies and intrigues were conducted in this holy and honourable office. Nevertheless the priesthood remained part and parcel of Levi's line; God had dedicated it to his service. Yet here we see all of them as enemies of God, all of them intoxicated by Satan and furiously resisting the world's Redeemer, who was the end of the law.

Note, therefore, that those who are highly and honourably placed should take care lest they fail to discharge their duties faithfully, and become like those who are enemies of God. In this respect we see how very foolish the papists are when they harp on the title and office of priest. Supposing God had commanded that there should be a pope – he did not! – and supposing he was to have his seat in Rome – even less true! Even if all this were so, the fact remains that in the person of Caiaphas and his kind we see that those who have been raised to honour may abuse their power. Let us not, then, be so silly as to waste our time over mere masks. However honourable a title may be, let God not lose his authority on that account, as happens with the papists who deny the whole of Scripture and pay homage to their idols. We must not allow God to be diminished for the sake of some man-made dignity: he must retain his sovereign rule. That is one point.

As for any offence which we might take if we were so inclined, remember what is said in Psalm 118, which our Lord had cited, that he is the stone of stumbling which the builders refused (Psa. 118:22; Matt. 21:42). Who were they who built the house of God and his church? The priests! At the very least that should have been the duty they discharged. Nevertheless they refused the stone chosen by God to be the chief foundation. And that stone, although rejected, was laid in the key part of the edifice. God, in other words, did not fail to fulfil what he had decreed in his counsel, by raising his only Son from the dead and by placing him all the higher, since he had earlier made himself as nothing.

When it is said that the priests sought false witnesses, this was not merely to help them fabricate a charge; it was to find a pretext which would overwhelm and oppress our Lord Jesus Christ. He had indeed uttered the words, 'Destroy this temple and in three days I will build it up' (John 2:19). These were the words which came from our Lord's lips. They are repeated by the witnesses who come forward. We might describe them as sound and faithful witnesses, yet the Holy Spirit calls them false, for they wickedly misinterpret the statement. Our Lord Jesus Christ was speaking of his body, which was the true temple of God's majesty. The material temple built in Jerusalem was only a representation, a shadow, as we know. But in Jesus Christ the fullness of deity dwelt, as Paul says, both bodily and in substance (Col. 2:9). So we should not simply consider the words which may be said in evidence, but the intention of the speaker.

There is a good and useful lesson here, because men, we know, are so prone to malice and falsehood that any excuse is good enough for them. They think they are absolved in God's sight when they falsely accuse someone in this way. We should not dwell only on what is said or on legal forms or ceremony: we must consider the merits of the case. Those who can always claim that the evidence they gave was strictly correct may nevertheless be counted as false witnesses before God, as we see here.

At this point Caiaphas says *'What? Have you no reply? Do you not see that these testify against you?'* Yet Jesus Christ is mute; he receives all these things in silence. We may think it strange that he who had just cause to refute this error says nothing against it. However, as we have suggested and as we will see later in more detail, Jesus Christ is not now there to defend his teaching as he did before. We need to be wise and to distinguish one circumstance from another. Our Lord, having fasted in the wilderness, was sent by God his Father to proclaim the message of the gospel. During all that time we see how staunchly he defended the doctrine whose minister he was. We know that he withstood all objections. That is how he discharged his duty, for he had been sent as a servant of the word. Here, on the other hand, there is something special to consider. He is to be the Redeemer of the world. Therefore he must be condemned, not for having preached the gospel but in order to suffer affliction for our sake, as one cast into the deepest pit. He must maintain our cause and represent in person all transgressors, all who are accursed and who deserve everlasting death.

Accordingly since this was the task assigned to him, and since he was to bear the burdens of all who had mortally offended God, our Lord Jesus said nothing. Though he faithfully defended the message of the gospel when his duty and calling required it, he remained silent when discharging the office of Redeemer, as if yielding voluntarily. Yet it was not for his sake that his lips were sealed; it was for ours, as our representative.

It is true that he does go on to speak, not to defend himself but rather to make the anger and rage of the wicked burn even hotter. He thus does not seek to escape death. Of his own free will he allows himself to be oppressed, proving that he had forgotten about himself in order to atone for us to God his Father. He thinks neither of his own life nor of his honour; he is not concerned about suffering shame and abuse before men, as long as our sins are blotted out and as long as we are released from condemnation.

Now the chief priest *bids him swear by the living God to say whether he is the Christ, the blessed Son of God.* He answers, *'It is so.'* They would see his majesty when it was much too late. Now when our Lord Jesus Christ speaks as he does here, it is not to incline the chief priest and all his men to kindness. He utters a threat in order to nettle them all the more, so that if earlier they were full of malice and cruelty, this will further inflame their passion.

Notice first of all how those who scoff at God and who are wholly in Satan's grip use religion as a deceptive cover. The chief priest appears to be doing his official duties by calling on Jesus Christ to swear by the living God. See how low men will sink when Satan has blinded them! He drives them to such extremes of insolence that they cease to have any reverence for God or any feelings of shame before men. What our Lord's reply to Caiaphas and the rest shows is that, if for a time he had made himself as nothing, his majesty is in no way lessened: he must always be known and acknowledged as God's only-begotten Son.

He had, however, a higher consideration in mind. He sought to assure us that, although he had humbled himself for our salvation, he had surrendered nothing of his heavenly majesty, and that he chose to be oppressed in the sight of men so that we might know that we were honourable in God's eyes. Our disgrace has been entirely set aside. It is because our Lord Jesus Christ was silent, refusing to defend his righteous cause, that our mouths are now opened and we are able to call upon God, as if we ourselves were righteous. More than that, he is our Advocate who speaks on our behalf. So if our Lord Jesus remained mute, it was so that he might now intercede for us with God his Father; and although we are no more than poor and utterly wretched vermin, we nevertheless have access to God: we can appeal personally to him and with full voice can claim him as our Father.

This is the truth he meant us to learn when he went on to say, *'Hereafter you will see the Son of man seated at the right hand of God's power.'* We should not take offence at the fact that Jesus Christ became as nothing, but must always consider the purpose which he had in view. Offering no resistance, he chose to be condemned so that we might appear before God's judgment seat freely and without fear. Let us therefore learn that, whenever the story of the passion is told to us, we should sigh and groan, since the Son of God endured so much suffering for us. Yet at the same time let us also tremble before his majesty until it should be revealed to us, and let us resolve that, when he comes, it will be to make us taste the actual fruit which he obtained for us by his death and passion.

Let us fear also lest we are among those whom he threatened when he said, 'Hereafter you will see …' For the wicked and the reprobate will discover how terrible is God's seat, and how great is his power when he rises up to destroy them. When Paul sets out to describe the condemnation of the wicked and those cursed by God, he says that they will tremble before his infinite majesty and will be terrified by his sight (2 Thess. 1:8, 9). Since this is so, we should humble ourselves before the Lord Jesus, and not wait until we visibly see the majesty he will display at his last coming. Let us by faith contemplate him today as our king, the head of the angels and of every creature, and let us welcome him as our sovereign ruler. Let us ascribe to him the honour due to him, knowing that because he is given to us by God his Father for wisdom, redemption, righteousness and holiness (1 Cor. 1:30), we must ascribe to him all praise, and must draw from him fullness that will truly satisfy. Let us be sure we pay this honour to our Lord Jesus Christ, even though we do not yet see his judgment seat. May we contemplate him with the eyes of faith, praying that God may enlighten us by his Holy Spirit and so strengthen us that we may call upon him in time of need. And may we be so lifted up above this world, above all thought and understanding, that we may exalt Jesus Christ today as he deserves. That, in brief, is what we must remember.

As for what was said concerning Caiaphas and the priests who condemned him to death, let us learn not to be amazed by the obstinacy of the wicked and of the enemies of the truth. This is teaching we sorely need today, for we see the great of this world loudly blaspheming against the gospel. In our very midst we see those who profess the gospel and who want to be known as reformed – gospel men, we might say – but who, like implacable demons or like devil-possessed beasts, denounce the gospel message. We do not have to go far to see such things.[1] Let us stand

[1] Calvin's efforts at thoroughgoing reform aroused substantial opposition in Geneva, chiefly led by members of the older families who resented the Reformer's influence and who would have preferred a more relaxed form of Protestantism. Until 1555 the dissidents held a majority in the city's councils and proved to be a constant thorn in Calvin's side.

strong, then, against these hindrances and let us always learn to glorify our God. Let Caiaphas and all like him spew out as many blasphemies as they will. Let them assert that Jesus Christ was worthy of death, and that we should say nothing about a fact so bad. Let them pollute the air with their vile, accursed blasphemies! But let us hold fast to the word of our Lord Jesus Christ. If nowadays his truth is falsely condemned by men, is brought into doubt, is falsified, corrupted or twisted so as to mean the opposite of what it says, he is strong and powerful enough to defend it. Let us therefore be patient as we wait for him to appear and to redeem us. Meanwhile may we all learn to humble ourselves and to give him all the glory, since he chose to stoop so low and to make himself as nothing for our salvation.

> Now let us cast ourselves down before the majesty of our good God, acknowledging our faults and begging him to make us feel them more and more, so that we may be led in true confession to seek the grace of our Lord Jesus Christ which we so much need. May we come to him as poor, hungry souls, and may we reckon up the priceless blessings he has won for us, so that we may feel how much greater is the debt we owe him, and be stirred up to give ourselves wholly to his service. May we come to hate our wrongs and our offences and learn to be ashamed of them. May God receive us in his mercy, and not allow us, once we have come to him, to turn aside. May we grow ever more in strength, despising the obstacles which the devil puts in our way. And may we continue to the end to confess his gospel purely, so that at the last day our Lord Jesus Christ may own and acknowledge us as his true disciples.

4

REPENTANCE AND REMORSE

Then they spat in his face and struck him, and others slapped him,
68 *saying, 'Prophesy to us, Christ, who is it that struck you?'* 69 *Now*
Peter sat outside in the courtyard, and a servant girl approached him,
saying, 'You also were with Jesus of Galilee.' 70 *But he denied in the*
presence of them all, saying, 'I do not know what you are saying.'
71 *And when he was going out of the door, another servant girl saw*
him and said to those who were there, 'This man also was with Jesus
of Nazareth.' 72 *And again he denied with an oath, 'I do not know the*
man.' 73 *After a little while those who were there came up to Peter and*
said to him, 'Truly you are one of them, for your speech reveals who
you are.' 74 *Then he began to curse and swear, saying, 'I do not know*
the man.' And immediately the cock crowed. 75 *And Peter remembered*
the word of Jesus, who had said to him, 'Before the cock crows, you will
deny me three times.' Then he went out and wept bitterly.

1 *When morning came, all the chief priests and elders of the people*
took counsel against Jesus to put him to death. 2 *And when they had*
bound him they led him away and delivered him to Pontius Pilate, the
governor. 3 *Then Judas, who had betrayed him, when he saw that he*
was condemned, repented and brought back the thirty pieces of silver
to the chief priests and elders, 4 *saying, 'I have sinned by betraying*

innocent blood.' And they said, 'What is that to us? See to it yourself.'
5 He threw down the pieces of silver in the temple and departed; and
he went and hanged himself. 6 But the chief priests, taking the pieces
of silver, said, 'It is not lawful to put them into the treasury, since they
are blood money.' 7 So they took counsel, and bought with them the
potter's field in which to bury strangers. 8 Therefore the field has been
called the Field of Blood, to this very day. 9 Then was fulfilled what
had been spoken by the prophet Jeremiah, saying, 'And they took the
thirty pieces of silver, the price set upon him by the children of Israel,
10 and they gave them for the potter's field, as the Lord had commanded
me.' 11 Now Jesus stood before the governor, and the governor asked
him, 'Are you the king of the Jews?' Jesus said to him, 'That is what
you say.' 12 And when he was accused by the chief priests and elders,
he was silent. 13 Then Pilate said to him, 'Do you not hear how many
things they testify against you?' 14 He answered not a word, so that
the governor was greatly amazed.

(Matthew 26:67–27:14)

According to Paul, the preaching of the gospel is a savour of life to those whom God calls to salvation, but a savour of death to the reprobate who perish (2 Cor. 2:16). Here, two noteworthy and memorable examples are set before us, showing that the death and passion of God's Son were for the salvation of one man, but brought condemnation upon the other. Peter's fall demonstrated that he needed to be rescued from the pit into which he had stumbled. He had done his best to banish himself from the kingdom of heaven and to cut himself off, like some rotten limb, from the church. Nevertheless he gained much from the death of our Lord Jesus Christ, even though he was unworthy of it. As for Judas, we are told that when he learned that Jesus Christ had been condemned, he hanged himself in despair. Now as we said before, our Lord's condemnation should have given him the courage to hope in God, for it is through his condemnation that we are forgiven.

It was necessary, then, for us to have these two mirrors, in order to better understand that the death and passion of God's Son avail us nothing, unless we are called by special grace to share in its fruit. It is not enough that our Lord Jesus suffered: the good that he obtained for us must be imparted to us and given to us to possess. This happens when we are drawn to him by faith. Let us, however, follow the thread of the story so as to have a better understanding of what it is all about.

We read that our Lord Jesus Christ was treated most shamefully in the house of Caiaphas. *They spat in his face, he was slapped and men mocked him, calling him by way of abuse a prophet.* We are told this so that we might know that what he suffered in his own body was for our deliverance, in the sight of God and of his angels. No one needs to spit in our face to bring us before God blemished and besmirched! We are, all of us, not only marred by our sins but full of infection. We are detestable. Here, then, is the Son of God, God's lively image in whom his glory and majesty are brilliantly displayed (Heb. 1:3). Yet he suffered such insults so that in his name we might appear before God to obtain grace, and to be reckoned and acknowledged as his children with all our spots and stains washed away. That is the first thing we need to bear in mind.

Turning to the fall of Peter, we learn that *a serving girl, seeing him, accused him of being one of Jesus' disciples, but he denied it.* Another maid came along and again he denied it. Then a number of people pressed him harder, *and he began to swear and utter a kind of oath*, as if to say, 'May I be damned, may I perish, may the earth swallow me up if I know him!' That is how Peter falls, not once but three times – failures so grave, so appalling that we ought to be terrified as we read the story. Yet we know how zealous he had been. Jesus Christ had praised him, and the name 'Peter' had been given to him to mark the solidity and constancy of his faith (John 1:42). He had been taught in so fine a school and had heard it taught: 'He who denies me before men, I will deny and disown before my Father' (Matt. 10:33). Even so we see how he stumbled. Each of us, therefore, should have cause to tremble, for if we are not upheld from on high, Peter's weakness is no greater than our own.

In the first place, then, we learn how frail we are as soon as God lets go of our hand. This is no story about a scoffer, a worldly man, someone who never tasted the gospel, who had no fear of God or any reverence for our Lord Jesus Christ. On the contrary Peter possessed outstanding gifts, for from the lips of God's Son came the words, 'Flesh and blood did not reveal these things to you, but my Father' (Matt. 16:17). The Spirit of God thus dwelt in Peter. Yet with whom does he have to fight when he denies our Lord? A serving girl! If some man had attacked him or if some important person had scared him, he might have had an excuse. It took only a serving girl, however, to get him to abandon the hope of life and of salvation. When we look at the figure of Peter we learn that God must give us strength every minute of the day, otherwise we cannot persevere. And although we may endeavour to draw near to God and may have done many brave things, in an instant we will completely change unless God continues to make us invincibly steadfast.

Accordingly let us learn to practise Paul's admonition, that the man who stands should take heed lest he fall (1 Cor. 10:12). Of course we cannot sustain ourselves. Let us turn instead to him who has the means. Meanwhile let us walk in all humility, as Paul says in another passage: 'Since it is God who in his unmerited kindness grants us to will and to do, be sure you work out your salvation with fear and trembling' (Phil. 2:12, 13). What he means is that all pride must be laid low – yes, and complacency too. When we see how much we need God's help in so many ways, is it not right that we should be on our guard and not presume on our own strength, but should be stirred up to call upon God morning and night, trusting in his protection and guidance? That is the first thing we should notice.

We should also reflect that, however small our trials may be, they would soon overwhelm us if God did not do his work of grace in us and put things right. Those who, when safe from blows, fancy that they are exceedingly bold, become quite desperate when the slightest breeze begins to blow! If, however, God helps us, we will hold fast however wild the storms that come. We remember the analogy drawn by our Lord Jesus Christ. A building which is on firm foundations and which is built of good materials will always remain intact, however fierce the flood; but anything built on sand will soon collapse (Matt. 7:24-27). When, therefore, we are grounded upon our God and when he firmly holds our hand, we can readily withstand dangers, however great and severe. Yet even if we had no enemy to fight against us, we would be vanquished at once if God were to withdraw from us or let go of our hand, as was the case with Peter.

Peter, however, does worse: he does not deny the Lord Jesus Christ once only; he repeats his denial as often as he is forced to do so. He does not care if he goes from bad to worse, to the point that he adds oaths, as if to say that God might justly curse and destroy him. What we learn here is that anyone who falls and who does not quickly rise to his feet as he ought to do, will always plunge even deeper to his ruin; he will finally perish unless God provides a remedy. Such is our human condition. We first persuade ourselves that we are wonderfully strong, which is why our Lord shows us by experience that we are not, and that it only takes a tiny breeze to bowl us over. Even so we tell ourselves that we can get back up again. On the contrary, we only aggravate our ills, piling mistake on mistake and completely losing our heads. If Peter had been tempted a hundred times a day, he would have denied Jesus Christ a hundred times or – why not? – a thousand! That is how it would have been if God had not had mercy on him. God spared him, not wanting to test him further. At any rate, the three falls which are described here are enough to show us a dreadful example. All the hairs of our head should stand on end when we see that for the third time Peter forgot himself, and acted so senselessly as to deny his very salvation. Observe, then, that if he had faced more temptations he would not have resisted them any better, and might have ended in the very deepest pit if God had not spared him further. That is how we should profit from this teaching.

We do not, however, hear these things in order to pass judgment on Peter and to condemn his cowardice. Admittedly we would be right to do so, but first and foremost we must receive instruction so that, conscious of our weakness, conscious indeed that we can do absolutely nothing, we should not be puffed up with pride and madly fancy that we are strong in ourselves. At the same time we should know that the devil has so many ways of contriving our ruin that he would soon get the better of us, since Peter stumbled, unlikely as it seemed. Remember finally that our Lord Jesus takes pity on us by not allowing us to be tested beyond measure (1 Cor. 10:13). For it is clear that, unless he sustained us in his goodness, our plight would grow worse and worse, and we would discover that, having committed one offence, we were ready to repeat it, endlessly. We must take note of all these things.

Luke records that after our Lord looked at him, *Peter went out and wept bitterly* (Luke 22:62). This last scene shows us, as I already suggested, that the passion of our Lord Jesus Christ had already had a powerful effect, in that it picked Peter up from so terrible a fall. Was it not miraculous that God should have compassion on him, and that he should obtain mercy after committing so detestable an offence? As we pointed out before, Peter could not plead ignorance as an excuse, as if he had only sinned a little by denying Jesus Christ. He had already been told that if he did not confess and testify to his faith before men, he deserved to be cast out from the presence of God's angels, and his name struck from the book of life (cf. Mark 8:38; Luke 9:26). Nevertheless he did not care if, by this vile and unnatural denial, he might redeem this wretched, fleeting life, and avoid being brought before the judges.

He is not closely questioned. A servant girl speaks to him, but even supposing they had wanted to treat him roughly, he would only have been beaten and thrown out like a common ruffian. Yet he forgets all fear of God. When we see these things, we should think harder about ourselves, remembering that God had to employ all the treasures of his infinite goodness so that Peter might share in the fruit of his Son's death and passion. The fact that Peter obtained forgiveness for so grievous an offence – as is made clear by his repentance – is a miracle which should fill us all with delight. Anyone who, after sinning, is cut to the quick so that he weeps and groans before God, most certainly obtains pardon. It is a sign that God has already received him and is reconciled to him. For repentance is a special gift which comes from the Holy Spirit, showing that God is merciful to us and does not want us to perish, but is drawing us back to himself.

This is what we find in Peter. It follows, then, that already the passion of our Lord Jesus Christ had been of benefit to him, and in a miraculous way, as I said. Notice, however, that Peter was drowsy and unthinking until he received a warning sign from Jesus Christ, which was that *the cock would not crow until he had denied him three times*. Now if Peter had not been warned he would have continued to wallow in his sin and to be plunged into perdition. We should therefore realize how much we need to be stirred up once we have done something wrong. If we were deprived of God's grace, if he did not urge us to turn back to him, we would surely remain a prey to Satan; we would be so mindless that we would have no misgivings or any genuine intention of returning to the way of salvation. That is another thing to consider when we think about Peter.

When Luke tells us that Jesus Christ looked at Peter, he reveals even more clearly that, if we are to turn back to God, it is not enough to be goaded or to have our ear pulled. Jesus Christ must turn his eyes toward us and look at us. True, here an actual gaze is meant, but although our Lord does not live visibly among us we may be sure that until he looks at us, we will be stupid and dull where our sins are concerned, and will never think of weeping or groaning even though we have provoked God's wrath. Although his bow is already bent and his sword unsheathed, we will always remain careless until our Lord Jesus shows us that he has not forgotten us and does not want us to perish, but desires instead to rescue us.

For this to happen, we should daily listen to sermons which exhort us to repentance. How much, however, do they really move us? We have any amount of salutary warnings. Does not every creature urge us to come to God? If our minds were well-ordered and possessed an ounce of wisdom, when the sun rises in the morning, does it not summon us to worship our God? Then too, if we think of how the earth and all the elements, the animals and the trees, fulfil their duty, they teach us to obey our God so that he may be glorified in us. Yet no one thinks of these things. The cock, then, crows in vain, and not only the cock: God makes all of his creatures sing high and low to him, exhorting us to come to him. More than that, he speaks with holy lips through his law, his prophets and his gospel, saying 'Turn back to me.' Nevertheless, we know how dull and dim-witted we are: we are more like freaks! Our Lord Jesus Christ must therefore look with pity on us, as he did on Peter, in order to get us to groan in earnest and to give proof of our repentance.

When Peter is said to have wept bitterly, it is to highlight the grief of which Paul writes in Second Corinthians, where he says that there is grief which leads to salvation, which we cannot avoid but which we must seek (2 Cor. 7:10). Although we always want to be joyful and never to get depressed, sadness is something we ought to feel. When God touches us with distress, our hearts should be deeply troubled if we have wronged him. Disquiet of that kind is meant to bring us ease of mind, and grief is meant to make us rejoice before God and his angels.

We will shortly see that Judas repented, but in a very different way. As for Peter, he wept to show how hateful his sin was to him and that he had turned back to Jesus Christ. Notice that *he went out and wept*. This was again occasioned by his weakness, for he was afraid to reveal his repentance in the presence of the public. Even so, by weeping in private he shows that he is touched by the offence he has committed. He does not want to play the part of the penitent with men as eye-witnesses but, on his own, he weeps before God. We ought to do the same, for if we weep only when men are present, we simply show ourselves to be hypocrites. When, however, we retreat into ourselves and examine our faults and sins, if we feel real distress, it is a sign that this is no pretence on our part and that we know who our judge is. We come to ask for pardon, conscious that it is for God to rescue from the pit those who are, in a sense, already lost and condemned. That is the lesson we should learn from the story of Peter's fall and three-fold denial. He deserved to be cut off from the kingdom of God, except that Jesus Christ displayed the power of his passion and death to bring him to repentance, as happened here.

Next we read that *the priests and leaders took counsel together to condemn Jesus.* Since this was not in their power, they took him tied up and bound to the governor of the country who had the right to judge, that is, to Pontius Pilate. The Evangelist goes on to say that Judas repented when he saw that Jesus Christ had been condemned. He threw his silver down, which was the price of his betrayal, at the same time confessing his offence. The priests, however, refused to accept the silver, but bought with it a potter's field which had been a place for making tiles, but was now disused and could not be tilled or sown with seed. They therefore bought the field in order to bury visitors there. This was by way of a pious gesture, for they said that *it was not lawful to put the silver in with the temple offerings.* Thus, says the Evangelist, *what the prophet had said was accomplished*: the thirty shekels, the price set upon God by the people of Israel, was used to buy the tiler's field.

Here we must reflect on a point we began to consider earlier. The death and passion of our Lord Jesus Christ do not produce their fruit in everyone: it is a special grace which God grants to his elect whom he moves by his Holy Spirit. And although they may have fallen, he lifts them up again. If they have gone astray like wandering sheep, he corrects them and stretches out his hand to bring them back to his flock. Now here we have Judas who has been completely excluded from the number of God's children. It was necessary that his condemnation should be publicly known, in a way that was obvious to all. Let us learn, then, to recognize in each and every thing the inestimable goodness of our God. For just as he displayed his love for humankind by not sparing his only Son but by giving him up to death for the sake of sinners, so too he reveals the special love he has for us when, by his Holy Spirit, he moves us to acknowledge our sins, makes us groan and draws us to himself in repentance. The access, then, which we have to our Lord Jesus Christ is none of our doing; it is because God governs us and is pleased to make his election known.

There are circumstances here which we do well to note. Judas was a disciple of Jesus Christ and had done miracles in his name. Yet what was the result? Let us learn to fear and to walk with trembling, fully entrusting ourselves to our God. We should ask him not to let us fall like this poor wretch, to our utter shame. And even if we did fall, may God by his power lift us up again and may we turn back to him – not with the remorse which Judas felt, but with true and sincere confession. For the wicked do their best to mock God; they are fond of their sins and they even boast about them. In the end they become as bold as harlots, as the prophets Jeremiah and Ezekiel said (Jer. 2:20, 3:1-3; Ezek. 16:25-34). Nevertheless God will make them feel their sins. Such will be their terror that they will cry 'Alas!', but it will not be to entertain any hope or to come before God's presence. They will be moved by fury; they will flee as far as they can and will try to pluck God from his seat. There will be nothing but defiance and a gnashing of teeth as they rise in rebellion against him.

We, however, must arrive at a different kind of repentance. We must not take fright at the thought that we cannot escape God's hand and judgment. Rather we must confess our sin and must hate it. But after that we must make sure that we draw near to God and answer his summons without having to be brought by force. Let us come willingly and do him homage, confessing that we deserve to perish, but being also assured that although we are guilty of a hundred thousand deaths, he will surely have mercy on us. That is what Peter's repentance was like. The repentance of Judas, on the other hand, shows that it is not enough to have some consciousness of wrong and some misgivings: we must be wholly brought back to God.

There is something else that we should note. Many people – almost all – delude themselves. Having with a single word confessed their faults, however serious these may be, they think that they are in the clear, as if to shrug the whole thing off. And if we make a fuss about it, they think that they have been greatly wronged. 'What?' they say. 'Didn't I own up to my offence?' This is all the price they are prepared to pay, as if God were a small child who can be placated with a laugh – a false laugh at that, full of hypocrisy and deceit. In any case that is the way men usually are. They try to appease God by one means or another in the same way as Judas is said to have repented. So when God admonishes us and makes us feel our sins, let us be careful that we do not stop there. That is not true repentance. This is the test by which we can tell whether we are really repentant or not: it is when of our own accord we again seek fellowship with God and when we do not shrink from being judged by him, provided, that is, he receives us in his mercy. This he will do once we have condemned ourselves, for the person who, before God and his angels and before men, judges and condemns himself, will be justified and absolved, since his one request is that God should look favourably upon him. That, in sum, is what we need to know.

It was important that Judas should have made this confession: its effect was to make the priests even less excusable. The Evangelist thus relates this story so that we might understand more clearly the blindness which Satan inflicted on all these reprobates, and so that we might take thought to ourselves. When God presents us with such examples of his wrath and vengeance, and shows us men who in some ways are absolutely mad, deprived of sense or reason, and who are so brutish that they rush on with hellish rage, it is so that we might each bow our head and realize that often we too might end up there, if we were not preserved by God's grace and goodness. Let us make sure that we do not fight against our consciences as the priests did, for all who harden their hearts against God will finally become so reprobate in mind that they will lose all reason; and having in God's eyes exceeded all bounds, they will also cease in the eyes of men to feel the slightest shame. It is only right, therefore, that their depravity should be made known to everyone, and that they should suffer such disgrace that all should abhor their villainy.

This is why the Evangelist records that when Judas came to return the money, the priests remained unmoved. True, they declared that it was not lawful to put it in the treasury chest, because it was blood money. This is how hypocrites try to keep up appearances as a cloak and cover for their wickedness, but all they do is mock God. They never come to him honestly and sincerely. They merely say, 'Oh, we won't put this money in with the holy offerings, since it is blood money.' But where did the money come from? The priests, we know, lived off the temple offerings, just as today in popery so-called prelates and churchmen gobble up the offerings and do not care about how they are used. So the priests are not concerned that the silver given to Judas was taken from the temple offerings; it means nothing to them. Yet now they hesitate to put the money back into the offering chest. At the same time they rebuff Judas and jeer at him, as if to say, 'Well now, this rascal betrayed his master. We don't care whether he did right or wrong, but to avoid sharing in his misdeeds and to keep our hands clean, we will buy a field for the burial of strangers.' It is as if they had fully satisfied God, who can ask nothing more of them, despite the fact that they are not really blameless. This is how hypocrites always seek to offer satisfaction, fancying that by these means they can redeem themselves. It is all a childish game.

We are told about this, however, so that when we do wrong we might truly acknowledge our faults and not beat about the bush, but freely and fully confess them. This is what we are taught here.

And all the while let us pray that God may remove the blindfolds by which Satan tries to deprive us of our sight, so that we no longer languish in self-delusion and try to excuse our sin. Instead, may we more and more strive to examine all our failings honestly in order to condemn them and rightly to confess them.

For the rest, we are also taught that God confounds the ideas of hypocrites, so that they fail in the end to attain their purpose. For the priests would have dearly loved to wipe their sin away by buying a field for the burial of strangers. God, however, worked to achieve the opposite objective, since the field had to be called the Field of Blood – the Field of Murder. It would stand as a perpetual memorial, as a word always on the lips of men, women and children, so that the odious crime committed by the priests should be known and made manifest each and every day. People would therefore say, 'There is the Field of Blood' – that is, the field bought for the price of betrayal. And who did it? The priests and leaders of the people!

So we see that when hypocrites attempt to hide their misdeeds and to disguise themselves, God uncovers their evil all the more: he makes sure that their shame is made known to everyone, and that each of us abhors them. This was why I said that we should resolve to reveal all our transgressions, that God may be pleased to bury them in his and his angels' sight, and in the sight of all men, once we have acknowledged them for ourselves.

The Evangelist concludes by citing a passage from the prophet, proving that this was not only said about Judas' sin or about the devilish obstinacy of the priests, but in order to condemn all the people. We therefore read, *Thus was fulfilled what was written by the prophet: the price set on God was thirty shekels, which was spent on the potter's field.* This verse comes from Zechariah, who compares our Lord Jesus Christ to a shepherd who, wishing to rule the Jewish people, has taken his staff or crook, called 'Beauty' (Zech.

11:7).[1] His meaning is that the state of that people could not have been better ordered, if only they had allowed God's hand to lead them. Could anything better be desired? What could bring more joy, more supreme blessedness, than that God should take care of our salvation and should be a shepherd to us? The mention of 'staff' signifies God's rule over this people. His staff was not a club with which to strike and smash; it served to guide and peacefully govern the sheep who were attentive. We read of a second staff which he took, as when the people were rescued from the Babylonian captivity. God again acted as shepherd to them, and ruled them in peace under his hand. At last, however, they proved so utterly thankless that he had to forsake them, saying: 'I see how it is. I am merely wasting time and effort on you.' And speaking as men usually do, he went on: 'Let's finish our arrangement. Pay me, and let me go.' Then they brought him thirty shekels. 'Is that all the wages and reward I am to get from you?' For in speaking of the thirty shekels he had in mind the offerings which were laid up in the temple.

This was an empty ceremony which the priests and Jews greatly valued, though practised hypocritically neither in faith nor repentance. It is the same today with the papists, who think that God is more or less beholden to them when they perform their many rituals and their beautiful devotions. Yet God calls all of this tomfoolery. 'What,' he says, 'is that all that I am getting from you?' 'Look,' they say, 'this is a shepherd's wage, and we're much obliged to you.' 'No, no! I can do nothing with that. Throw it into the tiler's field. Use it for patching up your cracks and holes, or for making tiles. I'm off!' It is as if he said, 'If the rain is getting into

[1] Zechariah 11 is a prophecy of judgment. Armed with one staff called 'Grace' (AV: 'Beauty'), and with another called 'Union', God's shepherd drives out the evil shepherds but, being rejected by the flock, he breaks the first staff, 'annulling the covenant with the people', and also the second, 'annulling the brotherhood between Judah and Israel'. He receives thirty shekels as his wages, and casts them 'to the potter in the house of the Lord' (Hebrew), or 'into the (temple) treasury' (Syriac).

your temple, have it repaired. As for me, I want no part or portion of you. I want to get far out of the way. And don't think you can placate me by offering me a drudge's wage! I'll have none of it!'

That, in short, is what the prophet meant. Now we know that what was foretold at that time was fulfilled in the person of our Lord Jesus Christ, who is our true God manifest in the flesh (1 Tim. 3:16). So it was important that this passage should be visibly proved true, and that Jesus Christ should be priced at thirty shekels only. Thus the people showed no gratitude at all to him who is the everlasting shepherd, and whom God had established over them.

It is certain that as long as the people allowed God to govern them, our Lord Jesus Christ fulfilled his office as their Mediator, even though he had not yet appeared in human flesh. Let us remember this, in order to be sure that if God has graciously brought us together under his hand, making us part of his flock and giving Jesus Christ to us to be our shepherd, we must not provoke him so as to grieve his Spirit and annoy him by our rebellion and ingratitude. Nor should we pay God off in small coin, as the saying goes, but because he gives himself to us, let us own him as our God and king. Let us dedicate our lives to him and not offer him payment which he will reject. We must present our bodies and souls to him, for it is entirely right that he should have complete supremacy over us and have full possession of us, seeing that he seeks nothing but our salvation.

And so our passage ends: *Jesus, being brought before Pilate, was silent. Pilate questioned him, saying, 'Do you say nothing?' But he answered not a word, so that the judge was much amazed.* We must above all be mindful that, when our Lord Jesus Christ appeared before an earthly judge, it was so that we might be freed and absolved from the condemnation which we deserved before our judge in heaven. We know that we cannot evade what was said by the prophet Isaiah, that every knee must bow before God (Isa. 45:23). Now since God is the judge of all the world, how could we exist before his face and majesty? Every one of us would be compelled to condemn himself one hundred thousand times. If we had lived for no more than a year on earth, one hundred thousand offences would already be ours, deserving condemnation. Every one of us has evidence of this engraved on his heart and is convinced of it. How could God, who sees much more clearly than we do, not condemn us many times over? Yet here is our Lord Jesus Christ who went to the bitter end, submitting to prosecution by an earthly judge, a faithless man no less, impelled by nothing but greed and self-interest.

If the Son of God stooped so low, we should know that it was so that we might come before God with heads held high, that we might be received by him and cease to fear and shrink from his judgment seat. It was so that we might dare to approach him with boldness, knowing that he will mercifully receive us. We know, moreover, that Jesus Christ has obtained authority, power and sovereign rule to judge the world. If he was condemned by Pilate, it was to help us come boldly to him, conscious that authority to judge has been given to him. If he remained silent, it was because he chose to bear our condemnation, and not to resort to law in order to justify himself. It was necessary for him, he knew, to be condemned in and for us. Although innocent and unblemished, he took all our sins upon himself. We should not wonder, then, that he kept silent, as if he had already been convicted. He could not have fulfilled the office of Mediator except by pleading guilty, and confessing that, as our representative, he deserved to be condemned. That is what our Lord's silence signifies. He remained mute, so that today with full voice we might call upon God, asking pardon for all our offences and transgressions.

Now let us cast ourselves down before the majesty of our good God, acknowledging our faults and praying that he may be pleased to touch us to the quick, so that, without hypocrisy, we may weep and groan before him. Great and grievous though our sins are, may we not be hindered by despair, but may we always reach out to him and make him our refuge. And since we are so mindless that in ourselves we cannot succeed, may he look with grace and pity on us, and with a merciful eye. Since he has appointed our Lord Jesus Christ to care for us, as a shepherd cares for his sheep, may he so gather us to himself that we no longer follow the way of perdition from which he has rescued us, but may we follow the right path to which we have been led. May we be careful not to provoke his wrath so that he leaves us and ceases to be our shepherd. May he instead sustain us by his grace, to the end that we may truthfully make our offerings to him, showing that he has not wasted his time by ruling and directing us, and may we respond to his holy calling. And because he has been pleased to draw us to himself and to choose us as his people and inheritance – although we cannot fulfil a hundredth part of our duty – may he nevertheless uphold us in his goodness, and always make the fruit of Jesus Christ's death and passion effective in us, until we are rid of all our sins and are clothed with that perfection to which he calls us even now.

5

THIS MAN OR BARABBAS?

He answered not a word, so that the governor was greatly amazed.
15 Now it was the custom at the feast to release to the people a prisoner,
anyone they wished. 16 At that time there was a well-known prisoner,
called Barabbas. 17 So when they were assembled, Pilate said to them,
'Who do you want me to release to you? Barabbas, or Jesus who is
called Christ?' 18 For he well knew that they had delivered him up out
of envy. 19 Also, as he was seated in the judgment seat, his wife sent to
him, saying, 'Have nothing to do with that righteous man, for in my
dreams today I suffered much on his account.' 20 But the chief priests
and the elders persuaded the crowd to ask for Barabbas and to have Je-
sus put to death. 21 The governor answered them, saying, 'Which of the
two shall I release to you?' They said, 'Barabbas.' 22 Pilate said to them,
'What then will I do with Jesus, who is called Christ?' They all said,
'Let him be crucified.' 23 The governor said to them, 'What evil has he
done?' But they cried out all the louder, 'Crucify him.' 24 Pilate, seeing
that he was gaining nothing, took water and washed his hands before
the people, saying, 'I am innocent of the blood of this righteous man.
See to it yourselves.' 25 And all the people replied, saying, 'His blood be
on us and on our children.' 26 Then he released Barabbas to them, and
after he had scourged Jesus, he gave him to them to be crucified.

(Matthew 27:14-26)

We saw previously that our Lord Jesus Christ offered himself as a willing sacrifice, that he might make amends by his obedience for all our iniquities and might blot them out. Therefore he chose to be condemned. That is why Scripture says that he did not reply to the accusations which were brought against him. He had ample reason to do so, but his lips remained sealed, as is said by the prophet Isaiah (Isa. 53:7). This was not only to demonstrate his patient endurance, but also so that we today might boast that we are righteous and blameless before God – however much our consciences accuse and condemn us – knowing that God has received us in mercy, and that all our faults have been removed by the perfection found in Jesus Christ.

Thus, by making no reply and by refusing to demonstrate his innocence, the Son of God won for us the freedom to boast openly that that we are God's children and are counted righteous in his sight. We might at first glance think it odd that, having kept silent, Jesus Christ should now claim to be King of the Jews. These two things seem contradictory. John, however, goes further. He tells us that Jesus Christ claimed that his kingdom was not of this world; he declared himself to be the Son of God, and also confessed that he had come into the world to uphold the truth (John 18:36, 37). Both these things, however, can be easily reconciled. It was necessary that Jesus Christ should declare that he was King of the Jews, in order not to reject the words of prophecy. He also had to assert that he was the Son of God, not in order to secure his pardon but to ensure his condemnation and so avoid a more drawn-out dispute. Observe, then, that when mention is made of his silence, it indicates that he did not seek to excuse himself. As to his own person, his lips were sealed, but he did not fail to make the requisite confession.

Accordingly Paul says that our Lord Jesus Christ made a good confession before Pontius Pilate (1 Tim. 6:13). If it had been a matter of arguing the case for his defence, the judge was already convinced of his innocence. Had he spoken he would have easily won, which was why Pilate was amazed. Nevertheless our Lord Jesus Christ was careful to testify to those things which God his Father had committed to him, not in order to teach, for this was not the place, but to confirm and endorse the truth which he had earlier proclaimed.

Notice, however, that the crime which appeared to have most upset the Jews was that he had fomented unrest by prohibiting the payment of tribute to the Roman emperor (Luke 23:2). This was sure to alarm the governor, a pagan who served as the emperor's envoy. It is certainly true that Jesus Christ declared that he was king, but not an earthly king, as we see from the fact that when the Jews sought to crown him, he withdrew and hid upon the mountain (John 6:15). Here again he puts paid to this slander which, by upsetting society and public order, might bring the gospel into disrepute. For he who came to call us all into the heavenly kingdom and to allow us to share in it, had no wish to abolish earthly kingdoms which he upholds by his might and power. To spare the gospel from this calumny, our Lord Jesus Christ therefore said to Pilate: 'My kingdom is not of this world' (John 18:36).

What indeed would happen if his kingdom were of this world? What would we gain by hoping in him, since our lot on earth is such a wretched one? Unbelievers have a far better time of it than we do, given the trials we have to bear. True, God applies the rod far and wide, and those who try their hardest to escape it are certainly subject to much misery and affliction. Nevertheless it is we who are disciplined more severely, for God's punishment must begin with his own house and church (1 Pet. 4:17). If, then, Jesus Christ was an earthly king, we would seem to be completely alienated from him. Yet supposing we had all the comforts we wanted in this world, and supposing that through God's Son we here had something like paradise, even so our life is but a shadow; it is short and fleeting. Hence it is necessary for us to know that our Lord's kingdom is a heavenly one, so that we may look to that life which is enduring and to which God calls us.

The kingdom of Jesus Christ lasts forever, because it does not consist of anything of this world where all is perishable. Let us learn, then, to bear all our adversities with patience, knowing that they do not lessen or diminish the grace won for us by our Lord Jesus Christ. In fact these are all helps to our salvation, as Paul writes in the eighth chapter of Romans (Rom. 8:28). And although we may be vexed and mocked, although we may have to suffer much abuse, endure hunger and thirst, limp with drooping wings and be assailed on all sides, we must tell ourselves, 'Even so, God accepts us.' It is as if God were to lift up our chin and say to us, 'Look up, and do not waste your time on worldly things.' That, in brief, is something we should bear in mind.

It was thus for good reason that, to confirm what he had said, our Lord Jesus Christ should add, 'To this end I was born and came into the world, to declare the truth', and 'whoever tastes the truth hears my voice' (John 18:37). We are therefore taught how important it is that the kingdom of Jesus Christ should be no earthly kingdom. If this had been a casual saying he would have quickly passed over it. Since, however, he declares that he came into the world to bear witness to the truth, he draws our attention to the message which we should ponder in our hearts, that, leaving behind the world and all created things, we must come to him who is our heavenly king. It is in him that we should seek the spiritual blessings which are imparted to us. May we enjoy them to the degree that he knows is useful to us for our salvation.

Accordingly, among all that for us sums up the gospel, observe this word: Jesus Christ came into the world to witness to the truth. From this we conclude that we will never be disappointed when we heed his teaching, because it is quite certain that whatever promise he has made to us, he will keep. So when David wishes to strengthen himself against all tribulation, he says that God's word is like silver refined seven times and thoroughly tested by fire (Psa. 12:6). Whenever, then, we begin to doubt the promises of our Lord Jesus Christ and are troubled and harassed – for the devil by his craft attempts to weary and discourage us – let us come back to this testimony, that our Lord Jesus came into the world to bear faithful witness to us. And today he gives actual proof that none of his promises is made in vain; none can fail. That is the lesson for us here.

John goes on to record Pilate's question, 'What is truth?' (John 18:38). It was not a desire to learn that made him ask the question: he did so out of spite and in mockery – a failing which we see in many people today. When we speak of God's truth, we mean the teaching of the gospel. That is how Paul defines it in the first chapter of Ephesians (Eph. 1:13), so that we are able to distinguish it from other forms of knowledge. Of course if we are told of something which has really happened, that is truth. But when God calls us to himself and seeks to take us out of this world and to help us reach the heavenly life, that is truth to the supreme degree. All else, by comparison, is nothing.

Think, however, of how much reverence people have for the teaching of the gospel. The wisest people in the world, or those reputed to be so, are so blinded by presumption that, when questioned, they retort: 'What? Have we lived so long in this world without knowing about the gospel, or anything else at all?' They are all ashamed when told that God's truth has been buried, and that we must look much more carefully into it. We hear the kind of jeers which fly around when that is said! So it was with Pilate. Because the emperor had sent him to Judaea to be his second-in-command, he feels greatly offended when told about a truth of which he knows nothing. 'Well then, can we really be so ignorant? Have we learned only lies and falsehoods? Can we not tell the difference between good and evil? As for me, I hold an official appointment. I stand in the emperor's place and represent him. Do you criticize me for not knowing the truth?' That was what Pilate meant. Puffed up like a toad with pride, he refuses to be thought of as someone who cannot tell right from wrong. So we do not see him waiting for our Lord's reply. He poses his question contemptuously, as if turning away to leave.

We too should beware. If today there are very many Pilates who will not attend God's school or allow themselves to be taught, thinking that they already know enough, let nothing stop us from coming to the obedience of faith and from accepting what our Lord teaches us and lays before us. Let us especially understand that truth does not grow naturally in our minds, futile and false as they are, and that we are plunged into darkness until God brings us forth. Truth thus surpasses all our powers of mind and understanding. God must be our teacher if he is to keep us from error, and we must be humble if we are to receive what he has to show us. May we hold fast to this precious truth, that though we may compass heaven and earth and think that we have learned everything, we can be sure that it is merely smoke, which will drift away until we are grounded in God's word which is certain and unchanging. That, in brief, is what we must remember.

We read in Matthew that, as Pilate sat in his judgment seat, *his wife sent word that he should not condemn Jesus, for she had been deeply troubled by many dreams.* We cannot doubt that God desired to testify in a number of ways to the innocence of Jesus Christ, as he had done through Pilate's own lips. It was not that God had not already determined what was to happen to his only Son. For Scripture to be fulfilled, he must be the sacrifice which takes away the sins of the world. Nevertheless he must be shown to be righteous and innocent, so that we might be all the more certain that he suffered the condemnation which our guilt deserved, and so that we might always be mindful of our sins in all that we are told about his death and passion.

Now Pilate sought to absolve the Lord Jesus Christ, for although he had supreme authority against which there was no appeal, he was in a foreign land; the crowd was disaffected, and despite having a garrison in the city he was worried by sedition. He tried to proceed by subtle and conciliatory means and thus to placate the crowd. So we read that *at the feast of the Passover, he was to release whatever prisoner the people wished.* He gave them a choice between Jesus Christ and Barabbas who, John tells us, was a thief (John 18:40). The other Evangelists describe him as a well-known offender, who had even committed murder and stirred up insurrection and riot in the city (Mark 15:7; Luke 23:19). The man, then, was a pestilence who should have been hated by all. Nevertheless the people shout: 'Release Barabbas to us! Let him be pardoned! Let Jesus Christ be crucified!'

The custom that a prisoner was released at the Passover shows us how far men will be led by their foolish devotions. It would seem that the feast was the more greatly honoured by the freeing of a prisoner, and that this was considered an act of worship to God. It was merely an abomination, for Scripture says that whoever justifies an offender is as guilty before God as the person who punishes the innocent (Prov. 17:15). Those whom God appoints to the seat of justice must be equitable, for in arming them with his sword God does not say to them, 'Do as you please.' His desire is that they take fatherly care of the people, and that they make sure they do not rise up and cruelly oppress others by misusing their influence and authority. They are to be merciful and compassionate. Evildoers, however, must be punished, according to God's command. Yet what do these men do? They believe they are honouring the Passover feast by offending God and by openly sinning against his word! This should serve to warn us that we are not to follow our own whims when it comes to honouring God: we must gladly comply with his will in every possible way. So let us not invent whatever devotions we like, but let us be content to do what God orders and commends. It is obvious that custom still has the force of law today. Whatever practice is commonly accepted seems to be allowable.

In any case God does not fail to condemn it. We see how grave an error followed. This perversion meant that Barabbas was preferred to the Son of God. At first glance we might think it strange that our Lord was reviled in this way, and that a thief and murderer should have priority over him; that Barabbas should find greater favour among men, and that Jesus Christ should have suffered such ignominy and disgrace. Was it not enough for God's Son to be crucified and to endure so shameful a form of death, in addition to his other cruel torments? For death on a cross was the way that thieves were punished. It was not like the gallows today, it was like the wheel. Was it not enough for Jesus Christ to be flogged, for men to spit in his face and to be cast into the deepest pit, without being held up as an object of abhorrence to all men?

If we judge these things by our own reason and only by appearances, we will be at a loss to comprehend. We must look higher up with the eyes of faith and come back to the point made earlier, that God was directing all of this by his counsel. Let us not dwell on what the crowd and Pilate did, but let us fix our gaze on God's unchangeable decree. In order to humble us more, he chose to bring his Son to utter destruction and to place him lower than all the evildoers in the world, since he was, as we will later see, crucified between two thieves.

After all this Pilate tried to allow our Lord Jesus to escape, but by a devilish method. He had him scourged, which was what punishment was called in those days. He would have liked to free him after he was scourged, as he might have done for some minor fault. That was how he tried to calm the crowd's unrest. If, however, our Lord had escaped by this means, what would have become of the gospel or of the world's salvation? The punishment which Pilate ordered would have been a mark of shame forever, as if the gospel were an unsavoury message, since the judge of that place had condemned it, and our Lord Jesus Christ would himself have been cast out. At the same time we would have perished, because there was no other way by which we could be reconciled to God except by the death of his only Son. Our Lord's death opens for us the way to life.

The devil therefore strove as hard as he could to prevent our Lord from dying. Yet who else but he urged the priests and others like them to hound Jesus Christ to his death? Truly, he worked like a madman. And just as God sends the spirit of the whirlwind and of fury upon all evildoers, so that they contend among themselves and are like waves crashing against each other, so the devil was carried away when he tried to blot out the memory of Jesus Christ and to prevent the redemption of humankind.

By God's design the lips of the judge himself bore witness to the innocence of Jesus Christ, who at the same time died as a sacrifice for our redemption. God has but one, single will, but it fills us with amazement. He has his own ways of working which seem so strange that, with downcast eyes, we must acknowledge that our Lord Jesus suffered not by the will of man, but to give us a pledge of God's boundless love, declared to us in Jesus Christ, and to teach us how precious our souls and their salvation are to him. Let us reflect, therefore, on these things.

John, in his account, relates that although our Lord Jesus Christ was scourged, the crowd cried all the louder for him to be killed; and when Pilate heard that Jesus Christ had claimed to be the Son of God, he was much affected, and even more alarmed than before (John 19:7-8). To his question 'Where are you from?', no reply is made. 'Do you not know,' he asks, 'that I have the power to pardon or condemn you?' (John 19:9, 10). Now it is very clear why the Jews brought this accusation against our Lord. True, the charge which might have most swayed the governor was the claim to kingdom and sovereign rule. However, when the Jews realize that their malice is uncovered and that Pilate understands that these are concocted falsehoods, they say, 'We have a law, according to which he must die' (John 19:7). This was a privilege reserved to them in order to avoid quarrels over religion. For the Romans were completely worldly: they gave only ritual service to their idols, and endeavoured to maintain their rule by allowing all to worship as they chose. So the cry goes up, 'He made himself the Son of God, and has thus blasphemed' (John 19:7).

If Jesus Christ had not been the Redeemer of the world, to claim to be God's only-begotten Son would have made him guilty of death. Scripture commonly speaks of us as God's children if he has adopted us by grace; and those who have received special grace, such as rulers and magistrates, are also called 'sons of God', though in a different sense (Psa. 82:6). Thus there is all the more reason why Jesus Christ should be called the Son of God, since he was anointed to perfection by the Holy Spirit's gifts and powers. Why, then, do the Jews accuse him? First, through their ignorance of Scripture: they do not know that he who was to be the Redeemer should be the living God made manifest. Having no understanding of Scripture, untrained in its use and their minds numb through carelessness, they brazenly demand that our Lord be condemned.

Similar recklessness is seen in all who are ignorant. Nowadays, when people cry 'Heretic!', it is not because they have proofs ready to hand. The stupidest people are so frenzied that they claim to be zealous for God's honour, but they have no idea how or why. Besides this, the question of whether Jesus Christ was the Messiah or not should have been investigated, but the Jews rejected him without any kind of enquiry. We therefore learn that if we want to be zealous in the way that God approves, we must make true knowledge our rule and be taught by his word. Unless we speak like scholars in God's school, we can rack our brains as much as we like, all we will come up with is Satan's follies. God is the only proper judge, and he reserves the right to teach us himself. Let us therefore follow his word with singleness of heart, and let us do so peaceably. Let that be the rule which governs our zeal. This is something we need to bear in mind.

Now when we read that Pilate was more fearful than ever when there was mention of God's Son, we notice that in this poor pagan some seed of religion was at work to move and unsettle him. His conscience was so troubled that he did not know which way to turn. He saw before him Jesus Christ, a man marred, whom he had already scourged and who endured much humiliation and abuse. He had been spat at and slapped in the house of Caiaphas. Here, in short, was a man despised and rejected by all. Nevertheless the mention of God touched Pontius Pilate and aroused in him feelings of fear and dread.[1] What if we were like wild animals? If, when mention is made of God, we are not kept on a tight rein, must not the example of Pilate condemn us on the last day? We know that there are scoffers, absolute devils who, if we tell them what God teaches or if we cite his word, do not care whether they accept or reject it. They block their ears and blindfold their eyes; their mind is wholly intent on other things. They

[1] As the next paragraph makes clear, the preacher infers Pilate's reverence from his feelings of fear recorded in John 19:8. In his *Commentary on the Gospel of John*, Calvin writes that 'Pilate is proof that men have, by nature, a feeling for religion which does not permit them, where divine things are concerned, to rush recklessly in any direction they like' (*CO* 47: 409). On this inborn 'seed of religion', see *Inst.* I.3.1, 4.1.

are so presumptuous that there is no way they will give anyone a hearing. That is how they like it. 'It's all been ordained for us,' they say. 'So let God get on with it.'

Is that so? Yet here is Pilate who never heard one word of God's truth, who despised the law and regarded all that the Jews did as a fiction – here he is, a man who worships his idols but who is nevertheless moved by mention of God and feels its pull. Is it because of some majesty or splendour that he sees in Jesus Christ? Not at all! It is the mention of God which elicits his reverence. How many will be condemned by Pilate's fear, who go on their own sweet way and who cannot be won over, even though God's name is set before them? They do not simply hear God's word in passing; they have the opportunity to be taught it and to have the testimony of Scripture pointed out to them. If they do not deign to think about it or to make any real effort, are they not wholly possessed by the devil? Do they not show themselves as monsters who have suppressed all seed of religion, since in defiance of nature they have stubbornly set themselves against God? That is the lesson for us here.

On the other hand we find that whatever fears men may feel, whatever impulses or perceptions might lead them to honour God, they are like lightning which passes before the eyes and immediately vanishes. What kind of fear did Pilate feel? It was not deep enough to stop him displaying pride so great as to reduce God to nothing. This is how it is with all who are not ruled by God's Spirit. Fear sometimes grips them so that they humble themselves before God; at other times they do not fail to toss their horns, forget themselves and blunt their consciences in order to do evil. We see this in Pharaoh, who at one time is terrified. 'Pray to God for me,' he cries (Exod. 8:8, 9:28, 10:17). And when he sees God's power clearly displayed, 'It is the finger of God,' he says, 'we must submit' (Exod. 8:19). But straight afterwards he is worse than ever. Pilate was the same. We are therefore warned that our fear of God should not be like a puff of wind; it should have good roots that reach deep into our hearts. What kind of fear, then, did Pilate have of God? The kind that made him even less excusable.

That is why God awakens sleepy consciences which try to throw off every yoke; he brings them back and forces them to think more carefully about themselves. Like it or not, they are obliged to acknowledge their poverty and to be conscious of their failings, however happy they are to indulge them. Whatever scruples the wicked and those who scorn God may have are summonses issued by God to remove any excuse for ignorance. But then they go and give themselves free rein, throwing caution to the winds and with nothing to keep them in check. Such a man was Pilate. To begin with he is deeply alarmed, but immediately after he reverts to his true nature. 'Do you not know,' he says to Jesus Christ, 'that I have authority to pardon or condemn you?' (John 19:10)

Here we must observe that, even if Pilate had been a thief, he could not have moved a finger unless God had given him power. How then can he dare to take so outrageous a liberty as to condemn or pardon on a whim, just as he chooses? It would be better if every thief in the forest were left entirely free to do his brutal work, than to place in so honourable a seat people who, with never a thought for conscience, delight to wield power and who sow confusion in the world. Hence it is clear, as I said before, that there never was a living root in Pilate; it was merely a puff of wind. So we must learn to fear God, being firmly resolved to walk steadfastly in obedience to him and to fight courageously against whatever might deter us. May we always be kept in check by the thought that we must not provoke the wrath of him who has absolute power over us. That, in sum, is what we must remember.

Notice, however, at the same time, that the boast which Pilate makes is a source of shame to him. His enemies could reproach him with nothing worse than this, that he is happy to be known as a man who cannot tell good from bad. He boasts about it! This shows us that the higher those who mock God seek to rise, the further they must fall to their destruction. God gives them over to so reprobate a mind that they glory in their iniquities, and they become abhorrent to both heaven and earth. What then must we do? Let us learn to glory in the good, and to consider what is lawful for us. Those who boast of being great most certainly provoke God, because often they have amassed wealth and reputation illicitly, through all kinds of evil, cruelty and extortion. It is as if they mean to defy God by boasting of such things. Someone who has committed robbery on every hand will say, 'These are the goods I've got.' But see how he sucks the blood of poor ordinary souls! He will say, 'It's mine, I got it.' Yes, but how? By cheating and by shady deals, taking from one, devouring another and turning all order on its head. Someone else who, out of self-interest and by illegal means, has risen to a place of honour, wants to be held in awe. God is thus openly challenged. Let us learn to glory in those things that he commends.

There is no room for boasting, as if what God has given us is ours to own. Our boast should rather be that God has been pleased to adopt us as his children, has given us grace to walk in his fear and gives us the strength to abstain from evil. These are the things in which we should glory. If we happen to be small and contemptible in the world's eyes, let us pray that God may give us patience, so that we prefer to live in this condition than to be raised high and to enjoy ourselves as worldly people do, who have such fun that nothing can hold them back. In boasting, then, we do not ask for more than God allows us, and we scorn everything that he reproves, however much the world applauds those who are high-handed and whose wickedness knows no bounds.

The trial concludes when Pilate, *seeing that he was gaining nothing, but that the people were growing more and more turbulent, washed his hands, saying, 'I am innocent of this man's blood.'* As we saw before, it was essential that our Lord Jesus Christ should be shown to be innocent, and that this should be attested by his judge's very words. For when it is said that Jesus Christ suffered under Pontius Pilate and was condemned, it is not enough to have heard the story; we need also to know not only that he was innocent, but that he is the source of all perfection and holiness. How, then, did he come to be condemned? For two different reasons, it appears. We read that he is the spotless Lamb of God, and as such it was necessary for him to be condemned as a sacrifice (John 1:29; 1 Pet. 1:19). The word 'lamb' indicates that he was to be offered up. And what does the law say about sacrifices? That they are for sin and its curse. That is why Scripture affirms that our Lord Jesus became a curse for us (Gal. 3:13). That is, he received the curse which our sins deserved. It is in this capacity that he was condemned. Yet it was important that he be acknowledged as having no spot or stain, and that we should behold his purity with our own eyes, to the end that, perceiving our sinfulness, we might recognize in Jesus Christ the mirror of all perfection, and might examine our faults and come to hate them, confessing that we would have been rightly condemned if he had not delivered us.

In taking the basin of water and in washing his hands, Pilate performed a meaningless rite, as if by this means he might clear himself in God's sight. He did not seek to excuse himself, but was trying to placate the excited crowd. He did not protest his innocence before God, but merely said to the people, *'See to it yourselves, for I am blameless.'* None of this, as I have said, excused him. He was not fulfilling his office as a judge, for he should have died a hundred deaths rather than fail in his duty. Supposing he was witnessing all the tumults imaginable, he ought to have been high-minded enough to do what he knew was right and proper. Yet on seeing the crowd so excited he lets himself be carried away. Nevertheless, despite himself, he cannot help but testify to the innocence of our Lord Jesus Christ, and with his own lips he pronounces him righteous.

Indeed he condemns him, but this should be of comfort to us, for we know today that when we are brought before God's judgment seat, it is not to be condemned but to be received as clean and blameless, since the blood of Jesus Christ was truly shed to cleanse our souls. It is to this, then, that we must look.

The Jews, however, were driven by Satan to cry, '*His blood be upon us and our children.*' Now they were God's inheritance, the elect, the people chosen from among all the nations of the earth. Yet they renounce that dignity, all the promises of salvation and the holy covenant which God had established with their race. So we see them deprived of all the blessings which God had previously conferred on them as Abraham's descendants. The blood of our Lord Jesus Christ had to fall upon them, to their utter shame and to that of all their lineage. As he had earlier told them, 'Your iniquity must reach its peak, and you will be made to remember the blood of the martyrs, from Abel to Zechariah, son of Barachiah, whom you recently slew. You have always been among the killers of the prophets, and you have warred against God and his word' (Matt. 23:31, 35). Thus did the blood of Jesus Christ, which was for the salvation of the world and especially of the Jews, the firstborn by right, cry vengeance against them.

Let us, however, be washed in his blood. Let us ask God to come upon us in a different way, on us individually and on our children, that we may be cleansed, for our sins make us abhorrent in God's sight. May we be made clean, and may we allow the blood once shed for our redemption to come upon us, that we may be sprinkled through the power of the Holy Spirit, as Peter writes in his first letter (1 Pet. 1:2). Let us beware lest we refuse the grace which God offers us, and which the Jews lost because of their ingratitude, provoking his vengeance more and more. May we today be ready to receive the cleansing of our Lord Jesus Christ which we can only grasp by faith. Let us pray to God that we may not receive this washing in vain, but that day by day we may be purged of all our stains. May God allow the purity won by Jesus Christ to do its work in us, until we attain his kingdom and are rid of all our sins and our corruption.

> Now let us cast ourselves down before the majesty of our good God, acknowledging our faults so that they may touch us to the quick and prompt us to run more fervently to the remedy set before us, the death suffered by God's only-begotten Son. Let us come with such repentance that we may obtain grace in his sight, not only for a day but for as long as we are in life or death. And may we be renewed all the while by his Holy Spirit, so that we continue to serve and glorify him as he deserves. May we cling wholly to our Lord Jesus Christ and seek to walk according to his holy word, for he died and rose that we might live and die in him.

6

NUMBERED WITH THE TRANSGRESSORS

*Then the soldiers of the governor took Jesus into the praetorium and
gathered the whole band in front of him. [28] They stripped him and put
a scarlet robe on him. [29] And when they had plaited a crown of thorns
they put it on his head, and a reed in his right hand; and they bowed
the knee before him, saying, 'Hail, king of the Jews!' [30] And they spat
on him and took the reed and struck him on the head. [31] And after they
had mocked him they took the robe from him and put his own clothes
on him, and led him away to be crucified. [32] As they were coming out
they found a man of Cyrene named Simon; they compelled him to bear
his cross. [33] And when they had come to a place called Golgotha, that
is, the place of a skull, [34] they gave him vinegar to drink mixed with
gall, but when he tasted it he would not drink. [35] They crucified him,
and having cast lots, divided his garments, so that what the prophet
had said might be fulfilled: 'They parted my garments among them,
and cast lots for my robe.' [36] And sitting down they kept watch there.
[37] They set up over his head this charge which was written: 'This is
Jesus, the king of the Jews.' [38] There were two thieves who were cruci-
fied with him, one on his right and the other on his left. [39] Those who
passed by reviled him, shaking their heads, [40] and saying, 'You who
would destroy the temple and build it up in three days, save yourself.*

If you are the Son of God, come down from the cross.' [41] Similarly the chief priests mocked him, with the scribes and elders, saying, [42] 'He saved others, he cannot save himself. If he is king of Israel, let him come down from the cross and we will believe him. [43] He trusted in God, let him deliver him now if he will accept him, for he said, "I am the Son of God."' [44] The thieves also, who were crucified with him, reviled him in the same way.

(Matthew 27:27-44)

Previously we made the point that the kingdom of our Lord Jesus Christ is not of this world. We need to ponder this fact more deeply still. We see the shame and taunts he suffered: instead of a royal diadem he had a crown of thorns, instead of a sceptre, a reed. Every possible indignity that could be devised for man was devised for him. If, then, we concentrated on the facts as told to us here, they could prove enough of a stumbling block to alienate us from our Lord Jesus Christ, and thus from all hope of salvation.

Now what we have to contemplate by faith is the spiritual kingdom of which I have just spoken. We will therefore conclude that, however much men may mock the kingdom of Jesus Christ, he never ceases to be precious both to God and to his angels. We must always remember that when men dealt with the Son of God this way, it was so that he might take upon himself the ignominy which we ourselves deserve. For what can we bring to God as long as we are defiled by our iniquities? It is because our Lord Jesus allowed himself to be spat upon, to be struck and roundly abused, that God today acknowledges and reckons us as his children. This is where our confidence lies.

We should always remember, too, that God wants us to feel our faults more keenly, so that we should shrink from them in disgust when we realize that the heavenly Father did not spare his only Son, but that he had to suffer much in order to make atonement and to obtain grace and pardon for us. Given the shame which our sins brought upon him, we ought surely to humble ourselves and to feel utter dismay. Nevertheless, as I said before, we must also take fresh heart, and be so well grounded in our faith that, when we come before God, we cannot doubt that our Lord Jesus Christ obtained grace for us in allowing himself to be reviled for our sake. He thus obtained glory and dignity for us in the sight of God and his angels.

Our text records that our Lord Jesus *was led to a place called Golgotha, that is, the place of a skull.* The Hebrew from which the word comes means 'to roll'. It has this sense because when a corpse decays the head is bare of all flesh and resembles a ball which rolls. The place was therefore called Golgotha, because that was where criminals were punished and where their skulls could be seen. We are reminded here of what the apostle says in the letter to the Hebrews, that our Lord Jesus Christ was taken outside of the city (Heb. 13:12). This commonly happened when sacrifices were made; they were burned and their blood was brought into the sanctuary to wipe away the people's sins. Such sacrifices were likened to a curse; they thus had to be cast well away.

The Son of God was, therefore, willing to take this responsibility upon himself, so that we might know that we have been truly delivered and absolved by God. When we think of what we were really like, we deserved to be rejected by God and to see his terrible vengeance displayed. We can obtain grace only by coming to our Lord Jesus Christ and by seeking refuge in him, since our burden was lifted when he became hated and accursed for our sake, that we might find favour with God and be pleasing to him. For although Pilate his judge pronounced him guiltless more than once, he had to accept in his own person all that was necessary for our salvation. He guaranteed our debt, and in each and every way went surety for us.

Because our Lord Jesus Christ was cast out as unworthy of human company, as one who was so vile that he could not be tolerated, let us learn to follow him and to renounce the world, as the passage in Hebrews urges us to do. And if we are to be derided, cut off as rotten limbs and regarded with abhorrence, let us bear it all with utmost patience and with heads bowed, until the day when our sorrow will be turned to joy and when God will wipe away every tear from our eyes. Then what we now think of as shame will be changed into glory for us, for it is certain that all that we suffer for our Lord Jesus' sake is nobler in God's sight than all the splendour of this world. That is all we need to know about Golgotha.

The Evangelist now adds that *those who passed by mocked him, particularly the chief priests, scribes and elders.* For what reason? *'If he is the Son of God,'* they said, *'let him come down and save himself. He saved others. If he is king of Israel, let him show it!'* Here we see how dreadfully blind these wretched men were. Possessed by Satan, they had neither insight nor discernment. We see priests who should have been messengers of God (Mal. 2:7). They had been appointed for this purpose, so that by their lips God's word and will should be made known. We see the scribes, men trained in the law, but who in seeking to destroy our Lord Jesus showed that they trampled on holy Scripture and the religion in which they gloried. When previously they had been told of the Messiah, they answered correctly that he would be born in Bethlehem (Matt. 2:5, 6). They should also have been warned and informed that the Redeemer who had been promised was to suffer this kind of death. There was nothing obscure about this: Isaiah's text was as clear as if the story of our Lord's sufferings had been related to them (Isa. 53:1-12). They ought thus to have known that there could not have been a better account than that provided by the prophet, even though he spoke well ahead of time. Then too, both

Daniel and Zechariah clearly state that God would gather his people together and restore his church, by having the Redeemer suffer every reproach and curse in the sight of men (Dan. 9:24-27; Zech. 12:10, 13:7).

How, then, can they abuse the Son of God when he is doing all that duty requires, as the prophets had clearly revealed? It is obvious that, in forgetting what once they had known, they have been carried away by Satan. We, for our part, should make sure that we walk in God's fear, and that having tasted his word we receive it with reverence, being obedient to Jesus Christ whom it sets before us. It is in him that we find fullness of blessing, provided we come humbly to him. But if we think we can sport with God, our temerity will be rewarded in the same way as happened to these poor wretches who were beside themselves with fury.

There is something useful, though in a contrary sense, that we might learn from their blasphemies. It was because our Lord Jesus Christ chose to be our king and head that he did not save himself. The enemies of the truth cried, 'Let him save himself if he is king of Israel!' Yet it was necessary for him to suffer in his own body to obtain salvation for us. Why did he not spare himself? Why did he endure so bitter and shameful a death? Because only by such a ransom could we be set free. Accordingly we must defy all of Satan's henchmen and all his evildoers who spew forth the blasphemies recorded by the Evangelist. We must be all the more certain that we truly have a king who put our salvation before his own life, and who suffered all that was necessary for our redemption. His one concern was to redeem that which was lost. There would have been no hope for us if God's Son had left us to our plight. He was swallowed up in death: that is where our deliverance lies. Thus if God now stretches out his mighty hand to help us in time of need, it is because Jesus Christ bore all things with patient suffering.

Our Lord Jesus Christ had, as it were, to be forsaken by God so that we might know that he watches over our salvation and is always ready to assist us when we ask him. At the same time, let us arm ourselves against the trials which come when the devil attacks us, hoping to persuade us that God has abandoned us and has turned his back on us, and that it is pointless to hope in him. At such times we should know that Jesus Christ is the perfect model for all believers, showing us the path to follow and our need to be made like him. He allowed these blasphemies to be hurled at him, yet he steadfastly resisted and so won the victory for us. So let us fight today whenever the devil attacks, for he seeks to overthrow our faith and to close the door that gives us access to God, as if he had entirely forgotten about us. Let us follow Jesus Christ and await the hour when God will stretch forth his arm to show that he is merciful to us and is our Father, even if he allows us to be cast down for a time. So much, then, for the taunts and jeers which were heaped upon our Lord Jesus Christ.

There were other taunts besides: *'He trusted in God: let him save him if he loves him!'* Already we see this in the person of David, who uttered these very words when he laments that his enemies have had cause to poke their tongues out at him and almost to put their foot upon his throat, reproaching him for his trust in God (Psa. 22:7, 8). This surely is the deadliest wound that Satan can inflict, for just as the life of man resides in the soul, so spiritual life resides in faith, in making God our refuge and in resting on his promises. If we are deprived of these, it is the end for us: we are lost and crushed. That was why Satan tried to overturn the faith which our Lord Jesus had in God his Father. True, he fought far more powerfully than we can, for he was not subject to unbelief. Nevertheless he felt the full fury that these trials contained. Just as earlier the devil had contrived these things, so now he repeats them through his human agents. He had said to him, 'If you are the Son of God, command these stones to become bread, and you will eat, for you are desperately hungry. Should you not try to see whether you have power or not?' (Matt. 4:3). Jesus Christ cannot have been unmoved by this, any more than he was unmoved when reviled for his trust in God. So although we do not have similar power to resist and might in fact fail, we should find strength in him, knowing that it was for us and for our gain that he conquered these assaults and overcame them.

His enemies continue to shout, however, crying, *'He saved others, but cannot save himself!'* Again we see how reprobate in mind they had become. Was not the fact that he had saved others a sure, unerring mark of his divine power? They were not unmindful that he had brought the dead to life. He had restored sight to the blind and had healed paralytics, the lame and even the demon-possessed. In every miracle that he had done he had displayed the great treasures of his goodness and power. Yet these things are still held against him. We see, therefore, how these poor madmen, with no one to coerce them, are their own judges and rob themselves of every excuse, so that when they come before the great judgment seat of Jesus Christ they will have nothing to plead in their defence: their own mouths will condemn them.

If our Lord Jesus Christ saved others, he could most certainly save himself, unless he preferred to put them before himself. What is it we witness here, if not a marvellous act of kindness by which he chose to be destroyed in the sight of men, that he might rescue us from destruction? He chose to suffer what we ourselves deserved, in order to discharge our debt. In a word, he surrendered all temporal salvation by not placing his own life first or by sparing himself, in order that we might be certain of our eternal salvation, and might have a guarantee and proof of payment. Our faith, then, should be all the stronger. And whatever the devil does to upset us and to hinder our coming to Jesus Christ, should serve to fortify us even more. Let us make the most of what we are shown here.

The devil naturally knows where our salvation lies, and he makes that his mark so as to deprive us of it. He knows that if he can succeed in making Jesus Christ offensive to us, we are done for. Experience proves this all too well. Besides, all the obstacles which the devil visibly puts in our way to turn us away from God's Son should help to make us stronger still.

I said before that, when we hear that our Lord Jesus saved others but not himself, that comment might, on our own understanding, make us feel a little disdainful toward him; we might even reject him and cease to hope in him. On the contrary, we should know that when the Son of God cared nothing for himself and his own life, it was because the salvation of souls was so dear and precious to him that he did his utmost to achieve it. It follows then that we, being firmly grounded in him, should call upon him, fully trusting that his suffering for us was not in vain.

Now when they say, *'This is the man who would destroy the temple and build it again in three days'*, they display the utmost malice by pretending that he threatened to destroy the temple. What he said was, 'Destroy this temple, and in three days I will raise it up' (John 2:19). He attributed the destruction of the temple to his enemies, not to himself. And when they crucified him, did they not know that this had already begun to be fulfilled? For they were not unaware that our Lord Jesus Christ had declared himself to be the true temple of God as to his human body, for since he is God made manifest in the flesh (1 Tim. 3:16), and since his divine being is joined to the nature he took from us – since, I say, all fullness of the Godhead dwells in him, his body indeed deserves to be called a temple, much more than the Jerusalem temple or any other under heaven. His enemies did all they could to destroy this temple, but he built it again in three days. They had not forgotten his words, for they later repeated them to Pilate (Matt. 27:63). It is obvious, however, that once the devil takes possession of men he makes them so mindless that they can no longer tell right from wrong. Rage so seizes them that they hurl themselves recklessly at God, as if they mean fully and deliberately to defy him. Since this is so, we are warned to walk all the more carefully in the fear of God, when we see how well he worked to show how truly Jesus Christ spoke, when he said, 'Destroy this temple, and in three days I will raise it up.' For in his death we see at first glance only ruin, for so it appears to men. By his resurrection, however, he made all things right. We ought, accordingly, to be all the firmer in our faith, having no regard for Satan or for anything he might do to shake us or to cause us to doubt.

We are told next that *they gave him vinegar to drink, mixed with myrrh and gall.* We may assume that this was in accordance with the custom of that time, in order to hasten the criminal's death. At any rate Jesus Christ tasted but refused to drink, for he knew that his hour had not yet come. Before the condemned were lifted up, it was usual to give them this to drink, so as to disturb the blood and help them breathe their last more quickly. This type of death was most cruel and they needed help to die. As we will shortly see, the bones of the thieves were broken so that they would languish no further. Our Lord Jesus, however, would not drink, showing that he was ready to accept in full obedience the part entrusted to him by God his Father.

The death he endured was hard indeed. Horrible as it was, there were the spiritual torments which we will speak about tomorrow if God permits. All this might well have prompted our Lord Jesus Christ to bring death as close as possible. Instead he was willing obediently to submit and to suffer until he was delivered without any human agency. These things we need to bear in mind.

As to the clause which says that *his garments were divided, and lots cast over them,* Scripture was fulfilled. David makes these same complaints and thus prefigures Jesus Christ (Psa. 22:18). It is true that he speaks figuratively when he says that vinegar and gall were put into his drink, that men divided his spoils and in his troubles pierced and distressed him even more (Psa. 69:21). Such is the way of cruel and ruthless men who seek to harass poor, afflicted souls who are totally exhausted. David therefore is using metaphors to describe his deprivation – his loss of wife, house, possessions and estates. In Jesus Christ, however, all these things are clearly seen. He was given gall and vinegar so that we might understand that David was merely his image, while he was the true Redeemer, promised before time began. Why, after all, was the kingdom set up in the house of David, if not for the promise that it would last as long as the sun and moon (2 Sam. 7:13, 16; Psa. 89:4)? There was thus the eternal kingdom, which is now firmly founded on the Redeemer. Those things which were portrayed in shadowy and symbolic form in David, of necessity found fulfilment in Jesus Christ, as we see here.

For the rest, the Evangelist relates that *the thieves who were with him also mocked him.* This is true of only one of them, as is clear from Luke who gives a fuller account (Luke 23:39, 40). This is a common way of speaking, as when we say: 'Even little children know that.' Though only one child is meant, the plural is used. Or else: 'That's a matter for the women', though there may be only one. Thus we read that our Lord Jesus was derided, mocked and blasphemed by all, even by the thieves. Hanging him between two thieves was meant to make his death more shameful still. This was the place where evildoers were usually put to death, but even this disgrace was not enough for them. The impression had to be given that he was worse and more hateful than all the bandits in the world. So they put the thieves on either side of him, meaning that he was the chief of them. Accordingly, as Mark recalls, the prophet's words were fulfilled, 'He was numbered among the transgressors' (Isa. 53:12; Mark 15:28).

Now if he had not been numbered thus, what would have been our place and standing in God's sight? We cannot obtain grace without righteousness. God must hate us and reject us, until we are righteous before him and cleansed of all our sins and stains. Can God deny himself? Can he divest himself of his holiness, righteousness and justice? As long as we bring him only our defilement, we must be abhorrent to him. How then could we be justified before him if Jesus Christ had not been numbered among the transgressors? We are thus delivered from our condition. God receives us and accepts us as if we were pure and blameless, because our Lord Jesus Christ suffered such shame and humiliation in the eyes of men. This is what we have to remember concerning the thieves.

Consider how Luke's story ends (Luke 23:40-43). One of the thieves reproaches his companion for his stubbornness. 'Isn't it high time you were humbled?' he says. 'You have been condemned, and the punishment you suffer is for your own misdeeds and offences. You are a man accursed, and although all your life you were so mindless that you enjoyed your crimes, you have got to start lamenting them now.' Anyone, however bad, who has spent his life in pleasure, not thinking that he can be called to account, and who scorns justice as long as he remains unpunished, will have to change his tune once he is arrested. 'Well,' says the thief, 'you're in real torment. God and men are calling you to account. Your uneasy conscience tells you that you are suffering for your crimes. Will you still go on defying God?'

What the thief says surely proves that he has been taught by God's Spirit. Soon we will see many more things beyond compare, yet in this man's words we already see what sort of teacher

God's Spirit is, when he instructs those who are completely lost and senseless, so that they not only acknowledge their wrongs and yield in order to obtain pardon, but are also able to speak like teachers themselves, like men long trained in holy Scripture. Is not the protest which this poor thief makes the foremost thing that we could say to anyone who is hard of heart and who continues to rail against God, when what he should be doing is submitting and coming to repentance? Whatever the case, his protest had the effect of stripping this man whom Satan possessed of every excuse. Now although his warning was of no benefit to him, it ought to be profitable to us. Let us learn, then, to fear God, even though he spares us, but especially when he beats us with his rod and makes us feel that we have wronged him. We should be all the more affected so that we groan, while remaining steadfast and patient in our afflictions as this poor thief was. Nor should we rise up in pride and anger as the other man did.

Moreover we see in these two men mirrors of the human race. We see the wretchedness which wraps us round. This life is a pit of misery, the fruit of our sins, for Adam's fall deprived us of God's blessing. Admittedly God in his bountiful goodness overcomes this curse, showing himself to be our Father in many different ways, by letting us experience his gentleness, love and care for us. Nevertheless we bear many marks of our sinfulness, and whether high or low we are made to see that we are all under God's curse, death being the end which is common to us all. So we languish in this world, prone to illnesses of every kind, suffering heat and cold and sorely troubled in one way or another. In short, when we have suffered endless misery, where does it lead? We must all return to dust and decay.

We know that there are some who are touched by God, so that the afflictions they bear are effective and help toward their salvation, as Paul points out in the eighth chapter of Romans (Rom.

8:28). Others become worse: instead of humbling themselves and being moved somehow to repent, they grow all the more bitter, at the same time provoking God's wrath and lighting a hotter fire which will consume them. These things we know. Thus let us view the two thieves as mirrors of us all, for from the greatest to the least we are all guilty before God. If we all suffer in common, who can boast of being innocent? Who can possibly absolve himself? We are over our heads in condemnation! We suffer rightly for our sins, yet we do not all confess them equally.

There are, as I said, those who grow worse and worse and who openly rebel against God. They gnash their teeth and foam with rage and cruelty; they will never accept their condemnation. Or else they take the bit between their teeth and display such wilfulness as if to say that God will never win or overpower them. In sum, when poor sinners own up, humble themselves and confess their debts, they should give glory to God, admitting that he deals justly and fairly with them, and that it is only right that they should allow themselves to be punished. When, I say, poor sinners come to their senses, we can be sure that this is God's hand at work, that he has touched them by his Holy Spirit, and that in them we contemplate his infinite goodness in rescuing from hell and perdition those who were without hope.

In this poor thief we see as outstanding an example of faith as ever there was. We ought, then, to thrill and marvel at this miracle wrought by God. Consider his plight. He is close to death, and suffers awful torment as he waits for someone to come and break his bones and to dismember him – torture so bitter and terrifying as to make him lose both mind and memory. He sees our Lord Jesus Christ hanging there, like him, and suffering the greater disgrace. Yet what does he say? He not only acknowledges his faults humbly before God, not only assumes the role of teacher, so as to bring his companion back to the right path, but makes a confession which, when we look at the facts closely, deserves to surpass all others. 'Remember me,' he says, 'when you come into your kingdom' (Luke 23:42).

How could he conceive in Jesus Christ the idea of a kingdom? Our Lord is hanging there on the tree, cursed both by God and men, for in the law God with his own lips had said, 'Cursed is the man who hangs on a tree' (Deut. 21:23). It was no accident, then, that this was where God placed his only-begotten Son. When, therefore, the thief sees Jesus Christ accursed by God and man, and in human terms sunk in utter despair, only through faith and in spirit could he fix on the idea that Jesus Christ was king. He was well aware of the things which might turn him away from the Son of God, and which might make him think that it would be foolish and wrong to trust in him. Despite that he calls him king, and sees him as such even in death. 'Save me!' he says, 'Give me life! Remember me! Only then will I be blessed.'

In weighing up all these circumstances, we can be sure that this thief's faith was as splendid as that of anyone who has ever lived. Let us not be ashamed to be his disciples, for the death of our Lord Jesus Christ will avail us nothing unless we stand condemned, as it were, in order to obtain salvation in him. God cannot absolve us unless we confess that we are full of iniquity and defilement. Since we are guilty before God and since our consciences judge and condemn us, let us not be ashamed to follow the example of the thief, who can be a sound teacher for us. And now that our Lord Jesus has ascended up to heaven and taken possession of the glory given to him by God his Father, so that every knee should bow before him (Phil. 2:10), let us not hesitate to commit ourselves completely to his care. Let us know that to be truly blessed, Jesus Christ must remember us, must guide us and, since he has been appointed our shepherd, must watch over our salvation, so that we may be safe under his hand and protection.

The miseries of this present life should not hinder us from coming to him. Let us bear them patiently. The thief's prayer was granted, as we see, even though he could not avoid suffering a hard and dreadful death. May we so prize the spiritual grace given to us in our Lord Jesus Christ, and daily offered to us in the preaching of the gospel, that it may enable us to overcome all the worries, obstacles, griefs, troubles and assaults which we might meet. May all our afflictions be tempered by the knowledge that everything can be made to work for our good and for our salvation, through the grace of our Lord Jesus Christ. Let that be clearly understood.

Nor should we forget our Lord's reply to the thief, when he says, 'Today you will be with me in paradise' (Luke 23:43). Although he had not yet risen from the dead and had not yet fulfilled all that needed to be done for our redemption, already he displayed the power and fruit of his death and passion. Its fulfilment lay, it is true, in the resurrection, but it was joined to his death and passion. We know that as he suffered in the weakness of his flesh, so he was raised in the power of the Spirit (2 Cor. 13:4). We know also that as he suffered for our sins to clear us of our debt to God, so he rose to justify us (Rom. 4:25). Since we know these things, let us come freely to him with readier hearts, and let us not doubt that when he graciously remembers us and hides us under the shadow of his wings, we are able to defy Satan, death and all misfortune, glorying in our very weakness. And although in men's eyes we may be wretched ruffians, let us nevertheless rejoice in God and in the taste which, by faith, he gives us of the heavenly life and of the inheritance he has so dearly purchased for us, and which, through hope, can never disappoint us.

> Now let us cast ourselves down before the majesty of our good God, acknowledging our faults and asking him to make us feel them more and more, so that, being touched by them, we may with greater earnestness repent of them and grieve for them.

May we so walk in his fear that he may be glorified in us. May we know the purpose for which we were redeemed, and dedicate ourselves in all holiness to him and to our great Saviour, who sanctified himself so that we might be partakers of his holiness. And may he graciously pour upon us the gifts of his Holy Spirit, that we may be cleansed of all the infirmities and corruption of our flesh.

7

IT IS FINISHED

Now from the sixth hour to the ninth there was darkness over all the
land. [46] *At about the ninth hour Jesus cried with a loud voice, 'Eli,*
Eli, lama sabachthani?', that is, 'My God, my God, why have you for-
saken me?' [47] *And some of the bystanders hearing it, said, 'This man is*
calling Elijah.' [48] *And one of them at once ran and, taking a sponge,*
filled it with vinegar, and put it on a reed, and gave it to him to drink.
[49] *But the others said, 'Wait, let us see whether Elijah will come to*
deliver him.' [50] *And Jesus cried again with a loud voice and yielded*
up his spirit. [51] *And behold, the curtain of the temple was torn in two,*
from top to bottom, and the earth shook and the rocks were split. [52] *The*
tombs also were opened, and many bodies of the saints who had fallen
asleep were raised, [53] *and coming out of the tombs after his resurrec-*
tion they went into the holy city and appeared to many. [54] *When the*
centurion and those who were keeping watch over Jesus with him saw
the earthquake and what took place, they were much afraid, and said,
'Truly this was the Son of God.'

(Matthew 27:45-54)

We noted yesterday that the taunts and blasphemies of God's enemies did not prevent the death and passion of our Lord Jesus Christ from displaying its power in the midst of men's ingratitude and contempt. All who had any standing or reputation among the Jews were present there. With loud voices they mocked the Son of God, but this did not stop him showing mercy to a wretched thief and receiving him into eternal life. The man's status should not be allowed to overshadow or diminish the glory of God's Son. If we protest that a poor thief cannot be compared with men who were leaders of the church, who were members of the priestly line chosen by God and teachers of the law, it is quite pointless to look for personal worth when we speak of the salvation we obtain through God's unmerited kindness. Instead we should refer to what Paul says: 'It is a faithful saying that Jesus Christ came to save poor sinners' (1 Tim. 1:15).

When, therefore, we think of the fruit of the death and passion of Jesus Christ, we should be thoroughly humbled, finding in ourselves nothing but poverty and shame, in order that God may pour upon us the treasures of his mercy, his only motive being that we have plumbed the depths of misery. Our faith should thus be all the stronger when we see this thief, a complete outcast, being suddenly called by God and allowed to profit from the death and passion of our Lord Jesus Christ, who suffered for the human race. In no way do we see God stretching out his hand to those who appeared deserving, who had some merit in themselves, who excelled others or were generally esteemed by men. God's goodness shines most brightly when he draws poor condemned souls from the depths of hell, and shows mercy to those cut off from all hope of life. This is what should point the way to salvation for us, because hypocrites, although confessing they owe something to God's grace, shut the door by their arrogance. They are so puffed up with pride that they will never yield to Jesus Christ.

So let us be certain, first and foremost, that our Lord Jesus Christ calls to himself poor sinners who feel only shame in themselves, and that his arms are outstretched to welcome them. If we think otherwise, we will never have it in our hearts to come to him. The salvation he has won is meant for the most wretched of men, provided they see themselves as such, are humbled, cast down and conscious of their guilt before God. It is this that gives us assurance, this that opens the way to our sharing in the righteousness offered to us here, and by which we obtain grace and favour in God's sight.

That said, the Evangelist records that *there was darkness from the sixth to the ninth hour.* Here he is following the style of the time. If he were speaking of the third hour, he would not mean three o'clock, but the first part of the day. There are two things we must notice here. First, the day was counted from sunrise to sunset, twelve hours in all, whereas we count twenty-four hours in a day, from midnight one day to midnight the next. So clocks worked differently: the hours in summer time were longer than the hours in winter; according as the days were longer or shorter, so too were the hours. The second thing to note is that they divided the day into four parts, three hours making up a quarter, and each quarter taking the name of the hour which began it. The time between sunrise and the second quarter they called the first hour. The second quarter which went up to midday they called the third hour. The sixth hour began at midday, and lasted for the next three or four hours. The last quarter lasted until sunset and the day's end.[1]

This is why one of the Evangelists says that Jesus Christ was crucified at about the third hour (Mark 15:25), while here it is said 'about the sixth hour'. Matthew relates that he was crucified between the third and sixth hour, and that he had been condemned by Pilate at about the third hour. Mark, when describing the time when Jesus Christ was led to Golgotha, is reckoning

[1] The point of this rather elaborate note is explained in the paragraph which follows.

from the end of the third hour, not from its beginning. He was thus on the cross until the ninth hour, when the day was already drawing to a close. It is likely, then, that our Lord Jesus Christ remained hanging on the cross for no more than three hours.

During this time we are told that darkness descended over all the land – the land, that is, of Judaea. It was not a general eclipse everywhere. That would have veiled the miracle which God wished to perform, since the eclipse would have been attributed to the natural order. Moreover not many people spoke of an eclipse in other countries, and those who mention it are rightly suspect. Here, then, the land of Judaea is covered in darkness. At what time? At about three in the afternoon, when the sun was not close, as we say, to its resting-place. There had to be darkness, therefore, contrary to the normal order, to fill everyone with dread and amazement. A number of people judge that this was done by God as a token of his abhorrence, as if he were calling the Jews to judgment so that they might somehow feel the enormity of their crime, or as if by this visible sign he wanted every creature to hide from so dreadful a thing as the delivering of Jesus Christ up to death.

In one sense, so far as the Jews are concerned, the death of our Lord Jesus Christ should be considered a dreadful crime. Theirs was so grievous an evil that it surpassed all others and was detestable in God's sight. If, indeed, we hate murders and suchlike, what should we say when we think of God's own Son? To think that men should have been so insane as to try to destroy him who is the fount of life, or should have risen to blot out the memory of him by whom they were created and by whose power we exist! Nevertheless the death of Jesus Christ was most certainly a sweet-smelling sacrifice (Eph. 5:2), since – a point to which we must keep coming back – it was meant for the reconciliation of the world. Furthermore, darkness descended in order that the sun might bear witness to our Lord's divine, heavenly majesty. Although at that very time he was not only abased and contemptible in the sight of men, and indeed was made as nothing, as Paul says (Phil. 2:7), the sun pays him homage and as a sign it remains concealed. Thus we are taught that, to deprive the wicked of every excuse, God desired that in his death Jesus Christ should appear as the sovereign king of creation, and that when Paul speaks in the second chapter of Colossians of his triumph on the cross, that triumph should have already begun (Col. 2:15). True, Paul here relates his triumph to the cancelling of the bond which stood against us and of the debt we owed to God, for in this way Satan was overcome. Even so, all this was already revealed in the sun's eclipse. The Jews were therefore convicted of grievous and malicious ignorance, as if all might see that they were somehow unnatural and in Satan's possession.

This is what we should recall when Scripture speaks of darkness descending on the land. Today, it is true, we are illumined by the death and passion of our Lord Jesus Christ. What way of salvation does Scripture show to us? How are we enlightened so that we can come to God, if not through the gospel which sets God's Son before us, together with the fruit and power of his death? Jesus Christ is truly the Sun of righteousness (Mal. 4:2), for by dying he obtained life for us. The Jews, however, were deprived of this blessing. By the veiling of the sun they were shown to be quite cast out, to have no message which might be profitable to them or to be useful for salvation. By their ill-will they tried to suppress everything which might have given them hope – hope which was to be found only in the Mediator whom they sought to do away with in their ingratitude. They were thus justly deprived of the light of salvation, and God's wrath was seen upon them.

At this point our Lord Jesus Christ utters the cry, *'My God, my God, why have you forsaken me?'* Both Matthew and Mark recount in Syriac our Lord's words, which come from Psalm 22 (Psa. 22:1). The Evangelists do not exactly reproduce the words as they occur in the Psalm. Matthew's 'Eli', which means, 'My God', appears in Mark as 'Eloi'. This is because the language had become corrupted. The Jews, as we saw some time ago, having returned from Babylon, no longer had a language as pure and whole as before. At any rate this cry of lamentation is taken from the first verse of Psalm 22. God deliberately chose this to be expressed in two languages, to show its importance and to draw our attention to it.

Now unless we imagine, as some madmen do, that Jesus Christ was speaking out of respect for the opinion of men, and not according to his own feelings and understanding, we must be deeply moved here, and absolutely amazed, that he here laments that God his Father has forsaken and abandoned him. It is much too gross and stupid to deny that he was gripped by anguish and heartfelt care, and instead to believe that he meant, 'People will think I have been forsaken.' Those who seek to distinguish themselves this way are not only ignorant, they are merely frivolous.[1] Besides they do not cease to blaspheme against God like mongrel dogs. Those who speak this way have no more religion in them than curs or brute beasts, for they do not know how much their salvation cost the Son of God; and what is worse they make light of it like the villains they are. So we must take it as certain that our Lord Jesus reached such a peak of anguish – yes, like those who experience the most excruciating torment – that he cried with a loud voice, 'My God, my God, why have you forsaken me?'

[1] The idea is found in Cyril of Alexandria's fifth-century treatise, *Concerning True Faith*, II.18. Here Calvin mounts much the same defence as in his earlier discussion of Christ's prayer in Gethsemane. Cf. his comment on Matt. 27:46 in *Inst.* II.16.11: 'His words came from deep bitterness of heart. Yet we do not mean to infer that God was ever either hostile or angry toward him. How could the Father be angry with the Son in whom he said he was well pleased (Matt. 3:17)? ... But we say that he bore the weight of God's vengeance, since he was stricken and afflicted by his hand, and experienced all the signs which God shows toward sinners when he is wrathful with them and punishes them.'

As we said a while ago, the story of his death would be cold indeed if we did not reflect on the obedience he gave to God his Father. Thus, when we want to be sure of our salvation, the main thing to consider is that, though we have committed many faults and iniquities and have often rebelled against God, all will be buried because our Lord Jesus Christ has justified us by his obedience and has made us acceptable to God his Father.

In what does his obedience consist, if not in the fact that, hard and awful as his death was, he surrendered himself to it? If there had been nothing adverse or difficult about it, it would not have been obedience. But by nature our Lord Jesus shrank from death, especially because it would be a frightful thing to find himself before the judgment seat of God, on behalf of poor sinners whose burdens he would bear. Even so he did not fail to stoop and to accept our condemnation. We therefore know that he showed perfect obedience, which gives us ample cause to glorify him. As the apostle writes in the letter to the Hebrews: 'He was heard for his godly fear' (Heb. 5:7). In any case, it was necessary for him to bear this hard and heavy load which was so contrary to human feeling. God his Father thus had to discipline him so that his obedience might be made known. Notice how the apostle insists that it was necessary for Jesus Christ to be struck with fear, otherwise we would not have known the cost of this sacrifice by which reconciliation has been made.

Peter also teaches that our Lord Jesus Christ not only suffered in his body but in his soul, when he says that he fought against the pangs of death (Acts 2:24). It is true that Scripture often declares that we have been redeemed by the blood of Jesus Christ, who offered his body as a sacrifice. This too is why his flesh is said to be food for us, and his blood spiritual drink (John 6:55). These things, however, are said on account of our ignorance. Because we are so coarse, the Holy Spirit points us to what in the death of

Jesus Christ is visible, so that we might have an assured pledge of our salvation. This, however, is not to exclude what we are taught in other places. It does not detract from the truth that our Lord's death and passion would not have availed to wipe the world's sins away, had he not been obedient to death, a dreadful death at that. Nor, as I said before, was he unfeeling in his obedience, even though he had to suffer great and extreme fears, yet all the while preferring our salvation to everything else.

This, then, is the lesson we must learn. The Son of God not only suffered in his body a most cruel death, but he was touched to the quick, having to endure awful conflicts as if God had abandoned him. He upheld our cause, having to experience the condemnation which rested upon miserable sinners. Our sins came between us and God, making God draw away from us. In a sense he rejected us. This is what marks us out as sinners. On the other hand Jesus Christ was never rejected by God his Father. Nothing could be clearer. Nevertheless he had to endure the pangs of death and he bravely fought to repel them, so that today the fruit of his victory should come to us. Remember, then, that when our Lord Jesus was in the direst distress, as if God had cut him off from all hope of life, it was because he was representing us, bearing the curse of the sins which separated us from God. For where can we find bliss, except in being quickened by God's grace and illumined by his light? He is the fount of all life and blessing, but our sins create a huge divide between him and us. It was necessary, then, that Jesus Christ should know and feel this.

Yet could he have entertained such fears, since in him there is nothing but perfection? That, we might think, would detract from the confidence he should have had, and from all that we should believe about him. He was without any fault or stain. There is, however, an easy answer to all of this. When he was tempted by Satan (Matt. 4:5, 6), he must, in keeping with his human nature, have indeed felt that he was on top of a high tower, but this did not lessen his divine power. We have every cause, then, to extol his goodness toward us, because he stooped to such lengths for our salvation.

And so he cried, 'My God, my God, why have you forsaken me?' There is no doubt that, being himself God, he could not have felt that this was so. No, but when he suffered, his deity had to give way to the death and passion which he had to bear. Hence his power kept itself hidden for a time, until he had done all that was required for our redemption. Notice, however, that this lament, this sentiment of fear which, in human terms, we are now describing, in no way diminished the trust which he had. As man, he always had confidence in God, as we discussed at length yesterday. He was thus the true model of real, perfect and full faith. Here we read that he was so distressed it seemed as if God his Father had forsaken him. Yet his faith was always perfect, and was not stricken or shaken in any way. Why then does he say, 'Why have you forsaken me?'

It is a natural impression. Here he is, then, according to the weakness of his flesh, feeling himself forsaken by God. Nevertheless he did not fail to trust in him. We see in his words two elements which might seem contradictory, and yet they match. The words which he repeats, 'My God, my God', reveal steadfastness of faith. He does not say, 'Where is God? How can he leave me?' He speaks directly to him. He must therefore be convinced and certain that he will always have favourable access to God his Father. There, I say, is sure and unerring evidence of the faith of our Lord Jesus Christ when, in this moment of crisis and anguish, he continues to call God 'Father', nor does he do so out of pretence. He was fully assured that he would find favour with him when he called upon him. Thus our Lord Jesus amply displayed his faith. But because the struggle was hard, as if seeking to defy all of Satan's trials and to reinforce his faith, he called upon God with the cry, 'Why have you forsaken me?' This is how it appeared to him as a man, for he had to plumb the depths, but not as a man vanquished. As Peter said, 'It was impossible for death to hold him' (Acts 2:24). Thus he triumphed in the midst of battle, which redounds all the more to his glory.

David experienced something of the same, for amid his afflictions, however great they were, he did not cease to call upon God and to hope in him. Yet because he was a frail man his faith was often unsettled, as he himself acknowledged (Psa. 73:2). What is special about our Lord Jesus Christ, as we saw last Sunday, is that all his feelings were well-ordered, because he was wholly righteous and free of natural corruption. This sometimes happens to us when our sorrows spring from a worthy cause, but our fears and worries are always in some sense at fault because our feelings are never undefiled. In our Lord Jesus Christ, however, there was nothing disordered or excessive. He was never in such deep distress that he failed to fix his hope directly in God and to call upon him, remaining firm and steadfast in the knowledge that he would be his Saviour to the very end.

Next we are told that some of those who were close by mocked him, saying, *'He is calling Elijah; let us see whether Elijah will come to help him.'* Some think that this was said by the soldiers who were ignorant of the law, but this is a foolish error. The soldiers knew nothing about Elijah. Without a doubt this was a blasphemy uttered by the priests who were expert in the law. Did they mishear our Lord's words, then? No! The name 'Elijah' is pronounced very differently from the word 'Eli', that is, 'My God'. A more familiar word could not be found and could not have given rise to any ambiguity. So it was out of deliberate malice and insolence that our Lord Jesus Christ was reproached for calling Elijah.

If we think that this is strange, would to God we did not see similar examples today! Nowadays the papists corrupt and misrepresent by their calumnies the things we teach, that is, which are taken from the word of God. They knowingly blaspheme to make our message hateful to many who are unschooled or who do not hear what we daily preach. Thus they falsely distort our words and twist them the wrong way round in order to give some credibility to their lies and to keep poor souls in ignorance. We see this not only in popery. Also among us there are rogues who accuse us of suggesting that Jesus Christ gave way to despair, simply because we say he suffered the anguish of death and was brought low, since on our behalf he bore the burden of our sins. These riff-raff profess the gospel, but keep on purposely blaspheming, thus proving that they are more worthless than those of whom we read here. So seeing today how the devil sharpens the tongues of his henchmen, and how men with brutish impudence spit out their venom against pure doctrine, we should not think it strange that our Lord Jesus Christ was vilified in this way. Let us patiently endure these blasphemies, asking God, as is said in Psalm 12, to cut off these vile tongues which are full of cursing and foulness (Psa. 12:3), and which seek only to blaspheme his name and cloak his truth.

Having told us that there was a vessel full of vinegar, mingled, as we saw, with gall, the Evangelist relates that *one who was there ran and took a sponge* – or as John records, a long branch of hyssop – *and gave it to him to drink.* John speaks more clearly at this point, for he tells us that Jesus Christ, knowing that all things were accomplished, said, 'I thirst.' Then he added, 'It is finished' (John 19:28-30). Notice that when this drink was given to God's Son, he did not ask for it as one who was thirsty. He had already refused it, as was earlier pointed out. Why? Because the drink was offered in order to shorten life. Our Lord Jesus, however, desired in every way to await his Father's time with quiet patience. That is why he did not want to hasten his death, but remained calm and obedient until all had been accomplished, although he had not yet yielded up his spirit, nor had he risen again. He meant that up to this time he had shown full obedience, so that now there was nothing to prevent him surrendering his soul to God his Father. That is how we are to understand this verse. Nothing now was lacking to complete our redemption except his departure from the world. This he was ready and prepared to do, and to yield up his soul to God. Given, then, that he had fully discharged his duty as Mediator, had done all to appease God's wrath toward us and had made satisfaction for our sins, he chose to accept this drink.

The saying, 'It is finished', is worthy of note and exceedingly important, for in uttering these words our Lord Jesus Christ is speaking of nothing ordinary or trite. What he means is that in his death we have all we need to come before God and to obtain grace from him. It is not that the resurrection is set aside. In effect he is telling us that he has faithfully discharged his office and that he has not come to be our Saviour only in part, but that he has fulfilled to the uttermost the duty entrusted to him, without in any way falling short of the Father's will. Therefore we are taught to fix our faith fully in our Lord Jesus Christ, confident that every part of our salvation has been accomplished in what he did and suffered for us. That is why his death is called a perpetual sacrifice, by which God's faithful people, his elect, are sanctified (Heb. 10:10, 12, 14).

Do we want to be quite sure that God is our Father? Do we want to be free to call upon him? Do we want rest for our consciences? Do we want full assurance that we are counted righteous, so that we are acceptable to God? Then let us abide in Jesus Christ. Let us not stray this way or that, but let us know that in him all perfection is found. Those, then, who look for succour elsewhere and who cast about them to make up for any deficit in our Lord's death and passion, deny outright the efficacy of what we are describing here. In a word, they trample his blood underfoot, for they dishonour him. As it is, among the papists what do we see but a denial of his death and passion? For as often as they set out to do good works – they call them merits – which they think will earn for them God's favour, they surely disavow the words of Jesus Christ, 'It is finished.' So in trying to obtain salvation before God and in wanting remission for their sins, to what do they turn but to their silly devotions? Each man plays the fool any way he chooses, so that all so-called devotions in popery set at naught what our Lord meant by the words, 'It is finished.'

What then is required? We must realize that there is not one atom of virtue or merit in us, unless we turn to that source which supplies them to the full. This is how our faith should be firmly fixed in our Lord Jesus Christ. We must above all be sure that, when he offered himself as a sacrifice, he did so to absolve us for ever and to sanctify us, as Scripture says, for all time (Heb. 10:14). Let this be the only sacrifice we need.

In popery, it is true, the devilish abomination of the Mass is called 'a daily sacrifice'. It is said that Jesus Christ indeed offered himself once as a sacrifice for the remission of our sins, but that each day it must be offered again. This is a most obvious blasphemy, in that they usurp the office given to Jesus Christ, who by God's oath was ordained to be our sole and everlasting priest for all time (Psa. 110:4; Heb. 7:21). Thus when mortal men take it on themselves to come before God and to offer Jesus Christ to him, do they not rob him of the honour which he reserves for himself alone, and which cannot be ascribed to any creature? So we see how these poor blind souls, thinking to settle their differences with God, provoke his wrath and vengeance by denying the death and passion of our Lord.

We should therefore extol God's grace all the more, since he pulled us from so deep a pit where, though seeking to draw near to him, we merely vexed him. We deprive ourselves of the fruit of Jesus Christ's death and passion when we look for any other sacrifice than the one he offered in his own body. We do well to remember this.

In conclusion it is said that *Jesus again cried with a loud voice, and yielded up his spirit.* What he said was, 'Father, into your hands I commend my soul' (Luke 23:46). From this we learn that our Lord Jesus Christ fought so hard against the pangs of death that he was at once victorious over them, and could boast as one who had overcome the most difficult trial of all. His victory belongs to us. That is, we may apply it to our use, for we are assured that not only did the Son of God fight for us, but that the victory he won is ours. Today, therefore, we need no longer fear death in any form, knowing that God's curse which held such terrors for us has been removed, and that death, which once had the power to wound us mortally, now serves as medicine to open to us the way of life. And just as before he had followed David in crying, 'My God, my God, why have you forsaken me?', he now utters the prayer said by David in Psalm 31: 'I commend to you my spirit' (Psa. 31:5).

David prayed thus in the midst of danger, as if to say, 'Lord, take me into your care, for my soul lies in my hands, bereft, while I am exposed to every kind of peril. My life hangs as by a thread. My only hope is that you keep watch over me.' Thus David takes God to be his protector, though he does not wait until death to call upon God and to trust him to save his elect, whether he upholds and defends them in this world or calls them to himself. For the chief and foremost protection that God provides is that, having called us out of this world and hidden us under his wings, he gives us his presence to enjoy, as Paul says in Second Corinthians (2 Cor. 5:8).

In uttering this prayer our Lord Jesus reveals that he goes calmly to his death, having triumphed in all the battles he fought for us. Already he exults in the victory won on our behalf, for our welfare and for our salvation. At the same time he shows that God is his Saviour who keeps his soul as a trust. For this is the meaning of his prayer: 'God, even after death you will be the guardian of my soul.' What he is really saying is that we cannot fail when we entrust ourselves to God, since he deigns to take charge of us, to support us and to keep us from perishing while we are under his hand. In making this plea we notice also that our Lord wins the privilege attributed to him by Stephen in the seventh chapter of Acts. For what does Stephen say when he is dying? 'Lord Jesus, I commit to you my spirit' (Acts 7:59). Stephen thus displays the fruit of Jesus Christ's prayer, so that now we can – indeed, must – come directly to him, confessing that since God his Father has made him our Shepherd, we should not doubt that we will be at peace whether in life or death, knowing that all things will work for our good and can be made to serve us. It is as Paul says: with Jesus Christ all things are gain to him, so that he cares neither for life nor death, since all is useful to him (Phil. 1:20, 21).

Let us learn, therefore, that when we are assailed by death, Jesus Christ has drawn the sting which could have mortally pierced us to the heart; that death can no longer harm us, and that when our Lord Jesus yielded up his soul to the Father, it was not only that he might preserve himself, but to ensure that our souls should be preserved by virtue of his prayer, provided we turn for help to him under whose protection we cannot perish, as he himself said (John 10:28).

Here, then, is the triumph of which we have spoken, and which already has done us great good. Our Lord shows us how precious is his death by turning directly to God his Father, that he might lead us to him and point out the way. The most essential thing, however, is that we understand the fruit which comes to us from his death, since he has torn up the bond which stood against us (Col. 2:14), and has made full satisfaction for our sins, enabling us to come before God his Father, no longer subject to death's injury and evil. And although we see in ourselves much which might alarm us and make us conscious of our poverty and wretchedness, let us nevertheless glory in him who humbled himself for us, in order to raise us up to him.

Thus, although while he hung on the cross he was an object of shame to men, God willed that by the lips of Pilate he should be proclaimed king. So while the world may revile his kingdom, let us not cease to make it our ground for boasting; and although, with him as our leader, we may suffer abuse, we have reason to rejoice. Our lot will be blessed indeed, because all the miseries, afflictions and disgrace that we bear are more honourable to God and more precious in his sight than all the sceptres, splendours and dignities which are so dear to men.

This, then, is how we must come to our Lord Jesus Christ and hold fast to him. Let us recognize the riches he brings to us. Above all, as he guides and directs us by his gospel, let us refuse all the comforts and ease of this world, so that we even come to hate them if they turn us from the proper path. In sum, may the Lord Jesus Christ have the honour which is his due, and may we ourselves not be like reeds which sway in every wind. Instead, may we be rooted in him, calling upon God and triumphing both in life and death, for the victory is already his. As long as we are in this world let us do him the honour of acknowledging that he alone can aid and uphold us. This he will do if we make him our refuge. Nor will he do it in any ordinary way, but miraculously; for although we may be plunged into deepest death, it is his office to rescue us, and to lead us to the heavenly inheritance which he has purchased for us.

Now let us cast ourselves down before the majesty of our good God, acknowledging our faults and praying that he may make us feel them more than ever. May we be so moved that they cease to please us, and may we turn back to God in repentance, not only for a day but with continual sighs and tears. And as long as we remain in this state of bondage, may our hearts nevertheless be raised on high, so that we come directly to God, knowing that he is mercifully inclined, that he gladly invites us to come and does not wait for us to seek him out. And since our Lord Jesus Christ has drawn near to us and shown us such love, abasing himself for a time in order to raise us up, let us continue to yearn for heaven until he gathers all of us in.

8

DEATH'S FIRST FRUITS

There were also many women there, looking on from afar, who had followed Jesus from Galilee, ministering to him; [56] *among whom were Mary Magdalene, and Mary the mother of James and Joseph, and the mother of the sons of Zebedee.* [57] *When it was evening there came a rich man from Arimathea, named Joseph, who also was a disciple of Jesus.* [58] *He went to Pilate and asked for the body of Jesus. Then Pilate ordered that it be given to him.* [59] *And Joseph took the body and wrapped it in a clean shroud,* [60] *and laid it in his own new tomb which he had hewn from a rock; and he rolled a great stone to the door of the tomb and went away.*

(Matthew 27:55-60)

As we saw earlier, our Lord Jesus Christ revealed the fruit and power of his death to that poor thief who seemed to be a lost, doomed soul. Yet the preaching of the gospel would have been vain and futile if all those who had earlier been taught the gospel and who had savoured it had backed away when they saw that the Son of God had died. The apostles, we know, had been chosen on the understanding that they would be like the first fruits of the church. We might therefore think that there was no point in choosing them to serve in this capacity. That is why we are told here that, although the apostles fled and displayed such base cowardice that even Peter denied our Lord, deserving to be cut off like some rotten limb from all hope of salvation, nevertheless God did not allow the teaching they had received to be extinguished or suppressed.

It is true that Matthew attests that it was the women who were steadfast, rather than the men. So we are led to praise God's goodness all the more, since he displays his power in our infirmity. In the same way Paul declares that God has chosen the weak things of this world, so that those who think they are strong should bow their heads and cease to boast (1 Cor. 1:27). If this were about the valour of men who had followed Jesus Christ to his death, we might regard it as normal. When, however, it is women who are led by God's Spirit and who act more boldly than the very men who had been chosen to proclaim the gospel throughout the world, we see how greatly God worked and how much praise must be ascribed to him.

We read, then, that *these women had followed Jesus, ministering to him.* This shows us more clearly still how willing they were to profit by the gospel. It was no small virtue that they had left their homes in order to move from here to there, suffering much hardship and shame. We know what our Lord had to face while he lived on earth. He tells us that foxes have their dens and young birds find a place to nest, but that he has nowhere to lay his head (Matt. 8:20). We also see that earlier these women had had the means to maintain themselves and to do so comfortably. When, therefore, they had such trouble in finding shelter, when they suffered hunger and thirst and were subject to many taunts, when everywhere they were harassed and driven out yet nevertheless overcame it all and bore it patiently, we can readily judge how much God had strengthened them. When confronted by death, they continued to hope in the Lord Jesus Christ. Yet such was their dismay that, had they thought that this was our Lord's utter end, they might have felt that he had deceived them. For he had spoken of the kingdom of God which it was his task to restore. He had spoken of fullness of bliss, and of the salvation which he was to accomplish. Where now were all these things?

Thus these poor women, bewildered and troubled as they were, not knowing what the outcome might be for our Lord Jesus Christ, remained calm nevertheless under his authority, finally judging that none of the promises he had made to them had been made in vain. So it was that they were waiting for his promised resurrection, although in human terms they might have thought the opposite. At the same time we learn that their faith was tested, and that we should not be overly worried if God seems to have forsaken us, and if all the promises in the gospel appear to come to nothing. These women, then, testify against us and put us to shame if we are found wanting in the fight. Could we undergo a more rigorous test than the one they endured? Yet, through faith, they were victorious.

Let us therefore arm ourselves when we are warned of Satan's attacks. Let us equip ourselves in advance, I say, and let us show that we rely on the power of Jesus Christ, so that although we do not at first see his promises fulfilled, we may continue to rest in him and to honour and revere him, knowing that he will be faithful in the end. We need to be thoroughly tested this way, otherwise we will be too delicate and our faith will grow weak, or else we will invent some earthly paradise for ourselves and our minds will not rise so high that we succeed in renouncing the world.

This is made all the clearer to us in the mother of James and John. Earlier she had been so driven by ambition that she wanted our Lord to take his royal seat with great pomp and pageantry, with her two sons as his lieutenants. 'Command,' she had said, 'that one of my sons should sit on your right hand, and the other on your left' (Matt. 20:20, 21). There we have a foolish woman whose head is full of dreams of glory, and who wants earthly triumphs for her children! Now, however, she has changed to a very different school. She sees Jesus Christ hanging on the cross, suffering such ignominy and abuse that the whole world is against him, and God himself seems to have cursed him and cast him off. Accordingly, when we feel dismayed so that our minds are gripped by fear and anguish, God uses these things to strip us of all earthly affection, removing everything which might stop us from rising heavenward to the spiritual life, for which we ought to yearn. This is impossible for us unless we are cleansed of all that holds us here below. That is what we need to remember about these women.

This is not to say, however, that there was no sign of men, for we know that our Lord spoke to John and entrusted his mother to him (John 19:26, 27). Here the Holy Spirit seeks to place a mirror before our eyes, to show that it was God who led these women by the power of his Holy Spirit, thus demonstrating his might and grace in choosing instruments that men considered frail and weak.

We see the same thing in Nicodemus and in Joseph of Arimathea (John 19:38, 39). Matthew, Mark and Luke, it is true, speak only of Joseph, because, as we read, *it was he who came to Pilate.* Nicodemus thus took heart, seeing that Joseph had taken the lead. Nicodemus was a highly esteemed teacher, while Joseph was a rich man of high rank, and as we learn a member of the council (Mark 15:43; Luke 23:50). Consider whether they had been zealous enough to risk death for the sake of Jesus Christ, and whether while he lived they had left their homes to follow him. Had they? No! But when he died God roused them and stirred them up, regardless of men's judgment. God thus effected a strange and wonderful change in giving Nicodemus and Joseph such boldness that they did not fear the people's fury when they came to bury our Lord. Previously Nicodemus had come by night, fearing the mark of ignominy (John 3:1, 2), but now in this last hour he buries our Lord Jesus Christ. God must therefore have given him new courage. He would have hidden, no darkness would have been deep enough; he would have been timorous and cowardly had not God corrected these faults in him. He greatly profited, then, from the death of our Lord Jesus Christ, who poured out the gifts of his Holy Spirit on these poor men. Earlier they had not dared to profess their faith or to bear witness to it. Now, however, they not only speak openly; their actions reveal that they would rather be regarded as accursed by men and be reckoned as Jesus Christ's disciples, than lose what they had obtained, the offer of free salvation.

This is why Scripture says that Joseph 'was waiting for the kingdom of God' (Mark 15:43; Luke 23:51). These words tell us that we are estranged from God and banished from his kingdom until he gathers us to himself, to make us his people for the sake of Jesus Christ. We perceive, then, how wretched is men's plight before our Lord calls them to him and consecrates them to God his Father. If this blessing is denied us, woe and shame to us!

Now it was a most noble thing to be looking for God's kingdom, for the Jews had become debased. From a human point of view there were many reasons why this was so. The prophets had said that, when they returned from Babylon, God would be their Redeemer, a worthy kingdom would flourish, a temple more glorious than ever would be built, and the people would enjoy every blessing. Life would be happy, there would be rest for all and all would rejoice in God, blessing his name and giving him the praise. That was what the prophets promised. Yet what was the people's condition? Their neighbours consumed and devoured them; they were harmed and harassed. Sometimes such tyranny prevailed that innocent blood was shed throughout the city. The book of the law was burned and even reading it was banned on pain of death. Such cruelty took place as is horrible to relate. The temple was filled with defilement. And what became of David's house? It was completely dismembered and everything went from bad to worse. So it was no wonder that, among a people so brutalized, so much given to its wants and ambitions, there should have been so few who kept to true religion and who did not lose heart. Those who suffered patiently and who were firm in the faith were a small and scattered remnant.[1]

This is what was said about Simeon and Anna the prophetess (Luke 2:25, 38). It was said also about Joseph of Arimathea. Well then, among so great a multitude, among the Jews in so populous a land, the Holy Spirit points to four or five as if to an exception, testifying that these were looking for God's kingdom. From this we learn that, when all is hopeless and confused, we must keep our gaze fixed on God, and because his truth is infallible and unchangeable, let us remain steadfast to the very end as we overcome all the shocks, trials and perplexities of this world. Although we may groan, let us continually look to where our Lord calls and invites us. Let us wait patiently for his kingdom to be established among us, and all the while let it suffice that we have the pledge given to us by his Holy Spirit, by which he confirms that he has freely adopted us. So when God shows us that he counts us as his children, when this is impressed on our hearts by his Holy Spirit, and when we have the message of the gospel daily sounding and echoing in our ears, let us be strong in the faith and let us not

[1] Calvin's account of the plight of the Jews concerns events of the intertestamental period. Following the Seleucid conquest of Palestine (200–198 B.C.), a vigorous policy of Hellenization was pursued, reaching its zenith under Antiochus Epiphanes, during whose reign factionalism flourished, the temple was profaned, Sabbath observance and sacrifices were suspended, circumcision prohibited and copies of the law destroyed. The resultant Jewish revolt is chronicled in the first two books of Maccabees.

faint, though things may so bewilder us that we can imagine none worse. That, in short, is the lesson for us here.

Attention might now be drawn to an event which John records before our Lord was taken down from the cross. His side was pierced to see if he had already yielded up his spirit (John 19:34). No one had tried to hasten his death, as had happened to the two thieves, but thinking that he was already dead they came to try him with the thrust of a spear. It was then that they knew he had breathed his last, so the soldiers were content with that. This might seem to us a rather minor detail, except that appeal is made to the witness of the law. Here John desires to prove that our Lord Jesus Christ was the true Passover lamb, since by God's providence and marvellous counsel not one of his bones was broken. For we read in the twelfth chapter of Exodus that the Passover lamb was to be eaten with none of its bones broken, and that it must remain whole (Exod. 12:46; Num. 9:12). Why was it that none of Jesus Christ's bones was broken? This was, as we know, the usual custom. No attempt had been made to spare him; he had even been placed between the thieves to mark him out as the most abhorrent, the worst of the guilty and the condemned. We thus see God working again to restrain the soldiers' hands. His will was that his Son should die yet be preserved, and that we should have clear evidence that he fulfilled the truth of that ancient sign.

Therefore we take him to be our Passover lamb who, when we are marked by his blood, keeps us from the wrath of God. We must keep coming back to this, that he is our Passover (1 Cor. 5:7). We must be sprinkled with his blood, otherwise the blood he shed avails us nothing. When, however, we accept his blood and sacrifice, and when through it we seek the forgiveness of our sins – knowing that we are wholly defiled until it washes and cleanses us – then we are sprinkled with his blood, a sprinkling done to our souls by the Holy Spirit. Then we are cleansed and God receives and welcomes us as his people, giving us assurance that although his wrath and vengeance are against all men, he looks with mercy on us and acknowledges us to be his children.

What we must remember about this verse, then, is that what was represented figuratively in the law has been fulfilled in the person of our Lord Jesus Christ. John goes on to say that 'water and blood came out of his side, and that he who saw it testifies to it' (John 19:35). The mention of water and blood reminds us that Jesus Christ brings us cleansing, and that by his sacrifice he provides the means by which our sins are blotted out, as John writes in his first letter (1 John 5:6). True, in death blood congeals, as is natural; and as well as blood there may also be water which is more fluid, not having the colour of blood which, being thicker, is held back. In any case what John teaches us is that God wanted us to see how much we gain from the death of his Son. In the first place, through the shedding of blood God has been appeased, since Scripture says that without the shedding of blood there is no remission of sins (Heb. 9:22). That is why from the beginning of the world sacrifices were offered. God declared that he would be propitious to all sinners who hoped in him. Nevertheless he desired that sacrifices be added, as if to indicate that forgiveness of sins would be free on our side, since we have nothing of our own to contribute, but that, to make amends, there would be a Mediator.

Thus the blood which flowed from our Lord's side bears witness to us that the sacrifice he offered makes up for all our iniquities, so that we are acquitted before God. Of course we ought always to feel guilty, so that we are humbled, brought to true repentance and stripped of all pride. Even so, we have the assurance that God considers us cleared and absolved for the sake of his Son, once we acknowledge our faults and offences. Why is that? Because his sacrificial death is sufficient to wipe away the memory of all our transgressions.

Now water signifies cleansing, so in order to be washed of all our spots and stains our Lord Jesus Christ willed that blood should come forth from his side, showing that he is our cleansing, and that we need look for no other remedy to rid ourselves of our defilement. He came to us therefore in water and blood, and through them we have fullness of salvation in him. We do not need to run round in circles or to look this way and that for help.

When we look more closely, we notice a strong parallel between the water and blood that came from our Lord's side, and the sacraments of the church, which are a confirmation and seal of what was accomplished by his death. For having suffered all that was necessary for our salvation, having fully satisfied God his Father, having sanctified us and obtained complete righteousness for us, he desired that the two sacraments which he ordained should bear witness to all these things. Two, I say – baptism and the Lord's Supper – for there are no more which he instituted in his word. All the rest is childish fantasy, and comes from men's temerity and recklessness.

Thus our Lord Jesus Christ displays the efficacy of his death and passion in both baptism and his holy Supper. In baptism we have the evidence that he has washed and cleansed us of all our defilement, so that God graciously receives us as if we were clean and pure when we come before him. It is not the water of baptism which has this effect. What could a perishable element achieve for the cleansing and purging of our souls? It is because of the water which came forth from our Lord's side. Let us go, then, to him who was crucified for us, if we want our baptism to be useful to us. To experience its truth let us direct our faith to Jesus Christ, who wants us to seek every part of our salvation in him, without straying or turning aside. Also in the Lord's Supper witness is borne that Jesus Christ is our food: under the bread he offers us his body, and under the wine, his blood. There we find all fullness of salvation when we are cleansed this way and when God accepts us as if we were just and righteous. We are therefore cleared of all guilt in his sight, for our Lord Jesus has made full satisfaction for us. This is how the sacraments should benefit us, as we place our trust in Jesus Christ and not look to any created being. This also should give us firm assurance concerning our Lord's death and passion. May our memory of them be daily refreshed, as God visibly shows how precious was the water and the blood which came from the side of Jesus Christ.

'These things were done,' says John, 'that Scripture might be fulfilled' (John 19:36). We thus learn that what was more fully said in earlier times was governed by God's secret counsel, and that although the soldiers did not know what they were doing, God had brought to pass the words uttered by both Moses and the prophet Zechariah. We have already spoken of the testimony given in Exodus (Exod. 12:46). John now adds what was said by Zechariah: 'They will see him whom they pierced' (Zech. 12:10).

In this verse, it is true, Zechariah is speaking figuratively. There God challenges those who scoff at his word and who are hardened in their rebellion and their wickedness. 'Well,' he says, 'they think they are waging war on those who preach my word and they think they can frustrate them by this means. But I am the one they are fighting against, so that when they despise and reject my word it is as if they were sinking their knives into me. So they will see the one whom they pierced.' This was truly fulfilled in the person of our Lord Jesus Christ, for his very body was pierced. Thus he was shown to be the living God who from the beginning had spoken by his prophets, since all that had been foretold was made manifest in him.

John further relates that Joseph asked leave of Pilate to take down our Lord's body from the cross, and to be given it for burial (John 19:38). He had a clean shroud and perfumed ointments had been bought – expensive ones, so John implies, of myrrh and aloes (John 19:39). *He laid him in a new sepulchre which he had made for himself, and which he had hewn from a rock.* Even in the grave our Lord Jesus Christ demonstrated the effect of his death. He was soon to enter into the glory of his resurrection, which God had determined to make known. Here again is absolutely reliable evidence that, amid so many bewildering events in this story which might upset us and shake our faith, we see God's incessant concern for his only-begotten Son as Head of the church and as his beloved. This gives us cause to hope in him. Yet we must also, since we are members of his body, wait for God's fatherly care to be extended to us and to all who hope in him.

We might perhaps wonder why our Lord desired to be buried in so costly a way, for it would seem superfluous to go to such expense over myrrh, aloes and the like. What advantage is it to someone who is dead to be washed, anointed and treated with so much ceremony? We might think that it is out of keeping with the message of the gospel, which tells us that we will rise at the last day through the measureless power of God. It would appear that lavishness of this kind should be refused and forgotten, and we might consider Joseph foolish in his devotion to the rite, since in a way it masks the hope of resurrection.[1]

Observe, however, that while Jesus Christ had done everything necessary for our salvation, the Jews continued with this type of

[1] The question of burial rites in sixteenth-century Geneva was complicated by the fact that, to counteract 'popish superstitions' such as vigils, processions and Masses for the dead, funerals were expected to be simply and modestly conducted. No church service marked the event, and the Genevan liturgy of 1542 contained no rubric for Christian burial. On the other hand, Calvin sometimes appeals, as he does here, to the universality of burial rites in order to demonstrate man's God-given sense of immortality, a sense dimmed though not extinguished by sin. Cf. *Inst.* III.25.5, 8.

ritual. Burial at that time was like sacrifices, washings and the lighting of the temple. It was necessary that in their ignorance this people should be brought up in the manner of children. Indeed everywhere on earth burial was regarded as sacred. God willed that it should be engraved on the hearts of men, even of the heathen, so that brutish though they were, men should have no excuse not to hope for a better life. Now although the heathen fell into error and will be rebuked for it at the last day, they took enormous care over the burial of the dead. There was no nation, however barbarous, which did not highly esteem such things. They did not understand why, any more than they understood the reason for their sacrifices. It served nevertheless to condemn them completely, since they had strayed so far from God's truth, and had perverted the testimony which he had given them in order to draw them to belief in the heavenly life.

Whatever the case, burial in itself has always been a mirror, so to speak, of resurrection. Bodies were placed in the ground and, in a sense, watch kept over them for a time. If there was no resurrection it would not matter if they were thrown out to be eaten by dogs or wild animals. But they were buried honourably to show that they would not perish even though they decayed. The Jews in particular had a number of ceremonies. The Egyptians, however, outdid them in very many ways, although this was merely for show, with loud lamentations, weeping and the tearing of hair. That was what the Egyptians did, but the devil had so bewitched them that they perverted all good order. As for the Jews who practised burial, this was meant to confirm their faith in the resurrection.

To return, however, to what I was saying before, Jesus Christ willed to be buried in the former fashion, for he had not yet fully accomplished our salvation in respect of the resurrection. True, when he died, *the veil of the temple was torn in two.* That was God's way of showing that this was the fulfilment and completion of all things, and that the symbols and images of the law could no longer continue. Nevertheless this was not obvious to the whole world, and there was no one capable of knowing that in Jesus Christ all the symbols of the law were at an end. This is why he willed to be buried. But enough said on that point.

We now know that by the resurrection of our Lord Jesus Christ, life has been obtained for us. So we should look directly to him, and not seek to be led by any other means than those he has assigned to us. We have already said that he appointed two sacraments in order fully to confirm our faith. If the Jewish manner of burial was necessary to us, our Lord would doubtless have chosen to make it permanent in his church. We must not, however, dwell on these earthly, immature elements. It is enough for us if our manner of burial is simple and ignores the perfumed ointments which stood for the resurrection now revealed by our Lord Jesus Christ. We would, therefore, stray from him if we relied on them for the poor teaching that they impart. We remember Paul's words, that our life is in heaven above (Col. 3:1-3). We must seek it in spirit and in faith, and must be united with our Lord Jesus Christ. Let us make him our aim, and become entangled in nothing which might make us turn aside, might hinder us or delay our union with him who is our Head, for his body is said to be the temple of God (John 2:21). This is what we learn from the story of the burial.

Scripture tells us that *he was laid in a new sepulchre.* This was a singular act of God's providence, for he could have been buried in a tomb which had long been in use. Joseph of Arimathea had forbears, and in so rich and prosperous a house as his to use a common tomb would be the natural choice. God, however, arranged things differently, desiring that our Lord be buried in a new sepulchre, where no one else had been laid. Rightly, then, is he called the first fruits of the resurrection (1 Cor. 15:20) and the firstborn from the dead (Col. 1:18).

Someone might object, however, that there were many who before our Lord died were allowed to partake of life. Lazarus was raised (John 11:44). We know also that Enoch and Elijah were taken without dying a natural death, and were received into imperishable life (Gen. 5:24; 2 Kings 2:11). Even so all of this depended on the resurrection of Jesus Christ. We must cling to him, then, as to the one who is the first fruits.[1] According to the law, the first fruits of the year were consecrated to God when no more than a handful of wheat and a bunch of grapes were brought to the altar (Exod. 22:29). When these were offered to God, it was considered that all the year's produce had been dedicated to him. The firstborn were similarly consecrated to God to demonstrate that all who were of Israel's line were holy (Exod. 13:12), and that God would accept them as his inheritance, having set them apart for himself and being content to have them as his people, just as a man might be content with his patrimony.

When we come, then, to our Lord Jesus Christ, we must acknowledge that in him we are dedicated and offered, so that death now gives us life and is no longer fatal to us. That is the significance of the 'new tomb': our Lord's burial must lead us to his resurrection.

Yet look for a moment at ourselves. Although everything which should help our faith has been accomplished by God's Son, and although we have evidence which should suffice, in our ignorance and weakness we are far from coming to Jesus Christ. Thus each of us should own up to his faults, turn to the remedy and not

[1] Calvin held that all the Old Testament saints were saved proleptically by the finished work of Christ. Cf. his *Commentary on Genesis* (Gen. 5:24): 'Enoch was not received into heavenly glory, but only freed from the wretchedness of this present life until Christ should come, the first fruits of those who will rise again. And since he was a member of the church, it was necessary for him to wait until all should go forth together to meet Christ, so that the whole body might be united to its head.' (*CO* 23: 108)

lose heart. We see what Nicodemus and Joseph did. They provide us with two examples we ought to ponder. The first is that they were not fully enlightened as to the fruit of our Lord's death and passion; they were in some ways ignorant and their faith was small. The second is that, at so critical a time and fighting against every adversity, they came to seek our Lord's body and to bury it, declaring that they hoped for the blessed resurrection which had been promised to them, and for which they longed.

Since this is so, though we may feel weak in ourselves, let that not stop us summoning up fresh courage. Of course we are feeble, and if God were to deal harshly with us he might well reject us. When, therefore, we think of our failings, we should know that God will accept our heart's desire, however imperfect it may be.

For the rest, since our Lord Jesus Christ has now risen in glory, although we must still endure much misery and wretchedness, and although he seems daily to be crucified in his members – for in truth the wicked do all they can to crucify him – let us not fail on that account, knowing that what we are promised in the gospel will not disappoint us. And although we may have to pass through many tribulations, let us look always to our Head. Joseph and Nicodemus did not have the same advantages as now we do, who are able to contemplate the Holy Spirit's power displayed in the resurrection of our Lord Jesus Christ. Despite this their faith was in no way weakened.

Because our Lord calls us to himself and loudly proclaims that he has ascended to heaven in order to gather us all together, may we persevere as we seek him out and follow him. Let us not grieve if we should have to die with him, that we might share in his glory. Paul exhorts us to be conformed to him, not only in his death but in his burial (Rom. 6:4; Col. 2:12). There are some who would be content to die with him for a minute or two, but they grow weary over time. That is why I said we must not only die once, and once only, but that we must allow ourselves to be buried to the utmost end. By 'dying' I mean suffering for his name's sake, for although we may not first be dragged to the flames nor condemned by men, when we are afflicted we suffer a kind of death which we must patiently endure. Because, however, we are not so quickly humbled, we must finally endure beatings, and that is when we must hold fast and go patiently on. For just as the devil never ceases to do everything he can to deter and corrupt us, so we must continually fight against him as long as we live. And while this is hard and upsetting for us, let us wait for the time when God will call us to himself and when we will never tire of confessing our faith.

In this respect we should copy Nicodemus, but not his cautiousness. For when earlier he had come to Jesus Christ he had hidden, not daring to show himself a disciple, even though confession of faith is required of us. When, however, he came to bury our Lord Jesus Christ, he made it clear and openly declared that he was one of the company of believers. So today we should follow his example of steadfastness. And although our Lord, together with his gospel, is odious to men and the object of their hate, let us see that we stick close to him. Above all, let us be sure that we will always be blessed and glad when God accepts our service, knowing that, even though we languish in this world, Jesus Christ did not attain the glory of his resurrection in order to leave us behind. At the right time he will gather us to him.

We should not wonder that our Lord rose on the third day: it was right that he should have some advantage over the rank and file of the church! Here also was fulfilled the verse of Psalm 16: 'You will not allow your holy one to see corruption' (Psa. 16:10). Thus the body of our Lord Jesus Christ remained incorruptible until the third day, for this was the end-time ordained and determined by the Father's counsel. We, on the other hand, have no end-time allotted to us, except the last day. So we should expect to languish for as long as God chooses. Finally, however, when the time is right, he will find the means of restoring us, even though we are no more. Paul exhorts us to this end when he calls Jesus Christ the first fruits (1 Cor. 15:20, 23). This is meant to restrain that fervent zeal which sometimes carries us to extremes: we would love to fly without wings, and it upsets us when God leaves us in this world and does not take us immediately up to heaven in a chariot of fire, as he did Elijah (2 Kings 2:11). In a word, we want to shout victory even before we have begun to fight! To resist this craving, then, and these foolish desires, Paul calls Jesus Christ the first fruits. We should be content that in his death we have a sure and certain guarantee of resurrection.

At any rate, because he sits at the right hand of God his Father, exercising all dominion both high and low, although his majesty is not yet manifest and although our life must still be hidden in him (Col. 3:3), let us think of ourselves as already dead and as living in this world like poor lost souls. It is therefore right that we endure all these things until our Lord returns. Then our life will be revealed in him, but at the proper time.

Such are the things we learn from the burial of our Lord Jesus Christ. Not only did he make satisfaction for all our sins but, as we will see, we are now acceptable to God, to whom we have access and on whom we can call in our Lord's name.

> Having this as our assurance, let us cast ourselves down before his holy majesty, praying that he may graciously accept us all, so that, poor and wretched as we are, we may continually seek refuge in his mercy. Although we provoke his wrath each day and rightly deserve to be cast out by him, may we nevertheless wait for him to display the fruit and power of the death and passion of his Son, by which we are reconciled to him. Let us not doubt that he will always be a Father to us, and will show that in his sight we are his true children by grace. Let our practice prove that this

is so, and that we desire only to be his people, for we have been bought with a price and must be made anew for his service. And although his Holy Spirit works in us, we are so frail that we cannot fulfill a hundredth part of our duty; we struggle and resist in the weakness of our flesh, limping along instead of walking as we should. May it please him therefore to rid us of our infirmities, and may we be united to him by that sacred bond which he has appointed – our Lord Jesus Christ, his only-begotten Son.

9

RISEN, AS HE SAID

On the evening of the Sabbath, toward the dawn of the first day of the
week, Mary Magdalene and the other Mary went to see the sepulchre.
2 *And behold, there was a great earthquake; for the angel of the Lord*
descended from heaven, and came and rolled back the stone from the
opening and sat upon it. 3 *His appearance was like lightning and*
his garments were white as snow. 4 *For fear of him the guards were*
terrified and became like dead men. 5 *But the angel said to the women,*
'Do not be afraid, for I know that you seek Jesus who was crucified.
6 *He is not here; he has risen, as he said. Come, see the place where he*
lay. 7 *Then go quickly and tell his disciples that he has risen from the*
dead; and behold, he is going before you to Galilee. There you will see
him. Lo, I have told you.' 8 *So they left the sepulchre quickly, with fear*
and great joy, and ran to tell his disciples. 9 *And behold, Jesus came*
to meet them and said, 'Greetings!' And they came and took hold of
his feet and knelt before him. 10 *Then Jesus said to them, 'Do not be*
afraid. Go and tell my brethren that I go to Galilee, and there they
will see me.'

(Matthew 28:1-10)[1]

[1] This is the earliest of the three extant sermons which Calvin preached on Matt. 28:1-10. The remaining two date from Easter 1559 and 1560, and may be found in Erwin Mülhaupt (ed.), *Psalmpredigten...*, pp. 83-99.

It might seem odd to us at first glance that, in order to give assurance that he had risen, our Lord Jesus Christ appeared to women rather than to his disciples. He did this, however, to help us see that he intended to test the humility of our faith. We must not depend on human wisdom; instead, we must receive with full obedience all that comes from him. Besides, there is no doubt that, in sending women to instruct them, he wished to punish the disciples, because when the crisis came, the teaching which they had received from his lips had been of no use to them. See how they all scattered! They abandoned their Master and were confused by fear. What had they gained by spending three years or more in the school of God's Son? Such cowardice deserved heavy punishment. They deserved to lose all the knowledge they had earlier acquired, since in a sense they had trodden it down and buried it.

Nevertheless our Lord had no wish to punish them severely. To show them their failings he chastised them gently, giving them women to be their teachers. Previously they had been chosen to proclaim the gospel throughout the world. They were in truth the first of the church's teachers. Since, however, they had been such cowards and had behaved so desperately that their faith almost failed, it was only right that they should know that they did not deserve to hear instruction from our Lord's own lips. They were thus referred to the women, until such time as they acknowledged their failings and until Jesus Christ had, by grace, reinstated them.

All of us are therefore admonished to receive the testimony which God sends us, even though the speaker may be lowly, a person without standing or reputation in the world's eyes. Now when a man is chosen or appointed as a notary or public official, whatever he does will be regarded as valid. No one will say one thing or another to contradict him, for the office he holds gives him respect among men. Will God, then, have less pre-eminence than earthly rulers, so that he cannot appoint whomever he likes to be his witnesses, or cannot expect us to receive what he tells them to say, without protest or dissent? This must certainly be accorded him, unless we mean to rise up against God himself. That is the first thing to notice.

Observe also that although our Lord appeared to women, who had the first place of honour, afterwards he himself bore ample witness to his resurrection, so that unless we shut our eyes, block our ears and out of settled malice seek to be hardened and senseless, we have abundant assurance regarding this article of faith. It is highly important. For when rebuking those who still doubted whether Jesus Christ had risen, Paul cites not only the women but Peter and James, the twelve apostles, and more than five hundred disciples to whom our Lord revealed himself (1 Cor. 15:5-7). What excuse, therefore, would we have for our malice and rebelliousness if we did not trust more than five hundred witnesses, purposely chosen not by men but by God's sovereign majesty? Nor was it only once that our Lord showed himself alive, but a number of times. It is also a fact that the apostles doubted, and their incredulity should strengthen our faith even more. For if, from the very beginning, they had believed in the resurrection of Jesus Christ, we could argue that it was all too easy. On the contrary, they were so slow that our Lord had to upbraid them for being confused and of little faith (Mark 16:14; Luke 24:25). They were so dull and so obtuse that they understood nothing.

Thus, seeing how hard it was for the apostles to accept this article of faith, we ought to be all the more certain, for if they were won over as if by force, we have every reason to follow their example. As Scripture says, 'Thomas, you have seen and believed. Blessed are those who believe without having seen' (John 20:29). When, therefore, we read that our Lord appeared to the women, think of what Paul says in another place: we should not dwell on who the speaker is and credit his message according to his rank or standing (cf. 1 Thess. 2:13); rather we must lift our eyes and minds upward, in obedience to God who deserves to have sovereignty over us and to make us captive to his word. For unless we are teachable we will never profit from the gospel message. To receive what God declares and testifies to us is not a mark of foolishness. When we have learned by obedience to benefit by being in God's school and by growing in faith, we will find that to submit to him is the fullness of all wisdom.

We turn, then, to the events recorded here: *Mary Magdalene with her companion came to the sepulchre on the first day after the Sabbath,* that is, the first day of the week. The Jews kept Saturday, which they called 'Sabbath', as a day of rest, which is what the word means. The following days of the week were called the first day after Sabbath, the second, the third and so on. And because for them the new day began after sunset, the two Marys are said to have bought perfumed ointments once the Sabbath was over, and had made preparations to come to the sepulchre the next day. There were not just two of them. John, it is true, only names Mary Magdalene (John 20:1); Matthew names the two Marys, and from Luke we learn that there were many more (Luke 24:10). These things can be easily reconciled. Mary Magdalene took the lead, and at the same time was closely followed by the other Mary. Quite a number, in fact, came to anoint the body of our Lord Jesus Christ. We are expressly told that they came to see the sepulchre, that is, to see if there was any way of gaining access and of entering. That is why these two in particular are mentioned here.

Matthew relates that *an angel appeared to them.* There were two angels (Luke 24:4; John 20:12), but because only one spoke, it is he who is singled out for mention. Finally, as the women were leaving, *Jesus Christ met them and sent them to his disciples*, telling them to gather in Galilee, where he would show them that he had risen. This was because the city of Jerusalem had through its wickedness denied itself his testimony. Admittedly, as time went on it did not cease to be a life-giving source, for the law came forth from it, as did God's word. Nevertheless our Lord did not choose to make himself known to his disciples in that city, whose wickedness was still fresh in the mind. Besides, he sought to accommodate the disciples' ignorance, for terror had so seized them that to see him would not have been enough if he had not drawn them apart, and shown himself in such a way as to give them absolute assurance.

We further see how the women named here did not fail to show their reverence for our Lord as for their Master, perplexed though they were by his death. We may, therefore, judge that God's word was still rooted in their hearts, for however weak their faith was they sought our Lord in the tomb. They nevertheless displayed a certain ignorance for which there was no excuse. They ought already to have lifted their spirits up, expecting the resurrection which had been promised to them, because the third day had been specifically assigned to them. They were so preoccupied that they forgot the most important thing, which was that Jesus Christ was to triumph over death and win life and salvation for us. That, I say, was the most important thing, because without it the gospel would be nothing, and our faith, as Paul says, would be wholly at an end (1 Cor. 15:14). Thus these women, whatever their affection for the Son of God and however much they knew the gospel to be pure truth, were so troubled and dismayed that they failed to understand that he must rise. Hence they arrived at the sepulchre with their sweet-smelling ointments.

They deserved to be censured, therefore, for their error, yet their service did not fail to be acceptable to God. He excused their fear until he gave them time to recover. From this we learn that when our Lord approves of the things we do, far be it from us to claim credit for them as if we were deserving. On the contrary, God in his unmerited goodness acknowledges those things which are unworthy of being offered to him. We would always have cause to condemn our works if God were to judge them strictly, since they are always marred by some spot or stain. Even so God spares us and does not cease to accept what we offer to him, feeble and faulty though it is, as long as it is wholly cleansed by faith, and as long as we recall that only in Jesus Christ are we acceptable to him. This is a point we need to grasp.

Consider too that in our Lord's tomb there had to be something far more fragrant and powerful than the ointments mentioned here. We said before that the Jews were accustomed to anoint the corpse, to confirm them in the hope of resurrection and the heavenly life. This was meant to show that bodies do not decay so much that they are not preserved until the last day, or cannot be restored by God. The body of our Lord Jesus Christ, however, was not to be subject to decay. The salves and ointments could not have brought this about: it was because Scripture had said that God would not allow his holy and gracious one to see corruption (Psa. 16:10). It was thus a miracle that the body of our Lord was preserved from all decay. Moreover because he was free of all corruption, we can now be sure and certain of resurrection glory, which we have already seen in him. The fragrance of our Lord's tomb and resurrection therefore extends to us: it brings us life.

What then remains for us to do? Let us no longer look for him in the sepulchre as these women did. We may learn from their ignorance and infirmity. Let us reach toward heaven, since that is where Jesus Christ calls and invites us. He has shown us the way. He has told us that he has taken possession of his heavenly kingdom in order to prepare a place for us, when by faith we seek him there (John 14:2).

Notice another detail which Matthew now adds. When the angel appeared, *the guards were terrified so that they became like dead men.* The women were similarly fearful, but the angel provided a remedy, saying, *'Do not be afraid. You seek Jesus who was crucified; he has risen, as he said.'* Here we are shown the love and zeal of these women. By the mouth of the angel our Lord corrects what he cannot commend. What I mean is that it is through his singular goodness that he accepts our imperfect service, which might well be abhorrent to him. He accepts from us that which has no value, just as a father accepts from his children things which might otherwise be considered silly and trivial. This, I say, is the generosity which God shows us. At the same time, however, he will not have us feeling complacent or indulgent about our faults. That is why he corrects these women's error. Their aim, though worthy, was condemned because it was faulty. Hence Luke relates that they received a stern rebuke: 'Why do you seek the living among the dead?' (Luke 24:5)

See also how the guards, who were wicked men and unbelievers, having no fear of God and without religion, were overcome by terror and behaved like madmen. The women on the other hand, though fearful, were immediately comforted. This is because we feel how frail we are when God reveals himself to us. Whereas before we were puffed up with pride and were so bold that we no longer thought of ourselves as mortal, as soon as God gives us some token of his presence we are bound to feel crushed. We clearly see our plight: we are no more than earth and dust, and all our virtues are mere smoke which drifts away and disappears. This is common to all of us, whether good or bad. Moreover when God frightens unbelievers in this way he leaves them as outcasts, since they do not deserve to taste anything of his goodness. That too is why they flee from his presence, why they fume and fret, gnash their teeth, lose all wit and reason and in their fury become as mindless beasts.

The faithful, on the contrary, once they experience fear, get back on their feet and take fresh heart, for God comforts them and makes them glad. So the fear which believers feel in the presence of God's majesty is but a prelude to humility, so that they may do homage to God as he deserves, knowing that they are nothing and that they must look to him for every blessing.

This, then, is why the angel says, 'Do not be afraid.' Attend to this word, for it is as if he said, 'I will leave these rascals to their confusion. They deserve no pity from me. I speak instead to you and bring you a message of joy. Because you seek Jesus Christ, be free of all fear.' Accordingly, let us learn to seek our Lord Jesus Christ, not ignorantly as these women did, but, having no reason now to seek him in the tomb, let us go straight to him by faith, in all sincerity. As we do so, let us know that this message belongs to us and is addressed to us. We must come boldly and fearlessly, not resentfully, though we must feel dread whenever we worship God's majesty. In any case we must not take fright as if moved by feelings of mistrust. Be sure, then, that the Son of God will meet us according to our measure when we come to him in faith. We will have ample cause to be comforted and to be glad, since it was for our gain and for our salvation that our Lord attained dominion and sovereignty over the heavenly life.

Next it is said that *the women went away with great joy and fear.* Again, the weakness of their faith is revealed. As I said, theirs was a worthy aim, but they did not keep to the proper path, as is shown by the fact that they were fearful. They could not gather their thoughts or make up their minds as to whether the resurrection was certain. They had heard it spoken of many times, but they could not master their feelings so as finally to decide that it was pointless to look for Jesus Christ in the tomb. That was the source of their fear. Their feelings were thus at fault. Of course, as I said, we should fear God in order to revere his majesty, to obey him and to be humbled, that he might be exalted in his glory, every mouth stopped and he alone accounted righteous, wise and all-powerful.

But from another point of view the women's fear was not good; it should be condemned, for it explains the dismay which these poor women felt. Although they could see and hear the angel, they had the impression that it was almost a dream.

From this we learn that God often works in us in such a way that we hardly know whether we are progressing or not. We are so ignorant that it is as if thick clouds were preventing us from coming to the true light, and we are ensnared by many fanciful ideas. In short, God's truth seems almost useless, yet there are some things about it which we savour and which make us feel that he has been at work in our hearts. So although we may only have a small spark of grace, let us not despair. Let us ask God to add to the smallness of what he has begun, and to help us grow in strength until we reach perfection, from which we are still a long way off.

The women, then, were overcome by fear mixed with joy. While this is censured here as a fault, it is nevertheless clear that God was all the time directing them by his Holy Spirit, and that the angel's message had not been brought to them in vain.

We must now move forward, to the verse where our Lord Jesus appears to them on the road and says to them, *'Do not be afraid, but go, tell my brethren that they must all gather in Galilee, and that there they will see me.'* From this passage we see even more clearly how the Son of God draws us by degrees to himself, until our faith is fully confirmed, which is what we need. It was already enough that the women had heard this message from the angel's lips, for he bore the marks that he had been sent by God: *his appearance was like lightning*. True, the whiteness of a robe or some such thing is not necessarily a vivid expression of God's majesty. The women, however, had sure evidence that it was not a mortal man who spoke but an angel from heaven. That evidence ought to have been enough. Nevertheless their assurance was all the greater when they saw our Lord Jesus Christ, whom they knew to be the Son of God, God's changeless truth. Here they had all they needed to confirm more fully what they had already heard from the angel's lips.

This is how we grow in faith, for in the beginning we do not know what power and efficacy the word of God contains. Well then, when we are taught we have some understanding, though very little, almost nothing. Gradually, however, God touches us by his Holy Spirit, so that in the end he persuades us that it is he who speaks. Thus we arrive at certainty, so that we not only possess knowledge but are so convinced that, although the devil does all he can to shake our faith, it remains unmoved. We hold firm to the truth that God's Son is our teacher, and that it is on him that we rely. He is in full control and deserves to have supreme authority over us. This is what we see in these women.

It is true that God does not work in everyone in equal measure. Some are drawn with such immediate effect that it is clear that in them God has displayed extraordinary power. Often, however, we will be taught in such a way that our ignorance and weakness will be all too apparent. This is so that we might be more mindful of the need to glorify our God, and might learn that we are indebted to him for everything.

Our Lord says to the women: 'Go and tell my brethren that they should go to Galilee.' In appearing thus to Mary and her companions, the Son of God did not intend to show himself to only seven or eight. He wished the news to be announced to his disciples, but also to be communicated to us, so that we might share in it. Otherwise how could the story of the resurrection profit us? When Scripture says that God's Son revealed himself this way, and wished its fruit to be proclaimed to everyone (Matt. 28:19, 20), it is much more tempting to our taste. Our Lord Jesus Christ wants us to be convinced of his resurrection, for all hope of salvation and all our righteousness lie in the fact that he rose from the dead. It is not that he did not cleanse us from our defilement by his death and passion, but he could not be left in such a state of weakness. He had to display the power of his Holy Spirit and to show by rising that he was the Son of God, as Paul says in the first chapter of Romans, and elsewhere (Rom. 1:4).

We should be assured, therefore, that Jesus Christ having risen, he now desires the way to be opened for us to come to him. He does not wait for us to seek him out, but has made provision for us to be called by the preaching of the gospel, and for this message to sound forth from the lips of the heralds he has chosen. So we know that today we may enjoy the righteousness which is ours in our Lord Jesus Christ, and may attain the heavenly glory, since he will not be parted from us. Accordingly he calls his disciples 'brethren', an honourable title which he reserved for those whom he had set aside to be his servants. He undoubtedly used the word to demonstrate the brotherhood he sought to have with them. Nevertheless it is a possession we have in common with them, as John declares (John 20:17). But we must also think of what is said in Psalm 22: 'I will proclaim your name to my brethren' (Psa. 22:22).

When, in Hebrews, the apostle relates this verse to Jesus Christ, he includes not only the twelve apostles as brethren: he applies the title generally, to all who follow the Son of God, and invites us to enjoy the honour (Heb. 2:11, 12). This also is why, when our Lord says, 'I go to my God and your God, to my Father and your Father' (John 20:17), he is not speaking of a small number, but is addressing the whole multitude of believers.

Now although our Lord Jesus Christ is our everlasting God, he does not cease as our Mediator to humble himself in order to be close to us, and to have everything in common with us, that is, in respect of his human nature. For although he was God's own Son, and although we are only children by adoption and by grace, this commonality remains, namely that he who is Father of our Lord Jesus Christ is, at the same time and through him, our Father, but in different ways. We must not rise as high as our Head. There must be no confusion here. If, in the human body, the head was not allowed to control all the limbs, it would be monstrous, a disorderly mass. It is right, then, that our Lord should retain supremacy of rank, since by nature he is God's only-begotten Son. Despite this, nothing stops us from being joined to him in brotherhood, so that we can call upon God freely and with full confidence. He will hear our prayer, because we have direct and intimate access to him.

We understand therefore the significance of the word 'brethren'. It means that today we share, by faith, this privilege with the disciples. Yet it does not diminish the might and majesty of the Son of God when he is thus joined to miserable creatures like ourselves, and consents to rank, as it were, with us. This ought to thrill us, given the great kindness which he shows us. In rising he obtained for us the glory of heaven, to attain which he also humbled himself and became as nothing (Phil. 2:7).

Since our Lord condescended to count us as brethren, that we might have access to God, let us seek him and freely come to him, for he graciously invites us to come. Consider indeed that he not only draws us to himself by his word, but also adds the visible sacrament, so that we might be led according to our littleness.[1] For however slow and frail we are, there is no excuse for our slothfulness when we fail to come to our Lord Jesus Christ.

[1] It will be recalled that this sermon was delivered on Easter day, one of four times in the year when the Lord's Supper was celebrated in Geneva. On such occasions Calvin invariably concluded his sermon with an explanation of the meaning of the sacrament and an invitation to partake worthily.

Here is the table prepared for us. To what end? Not to satisfy our bodies and bellies, though even in such things God reveals his fatherly concern for us, and our Lord Jesus Christ shows that he is truly the life of the world. Thus when every day we take our meals and refreshment, it is as if Jesus Christ were demonstrating his goodness.

There is, however, something special to bear in mind about the table set before us. It reveals that we are brethren of our Lord Jesus Christ, since he is one with us, as we read in the seventeenth chapter of John (John 17:21). He has also made us one with God his Father, and he declares that he is also our food and drink, for we are fed with his true substance, that we might have our spiritual life in him. That means more than if he were to call us brethren a hundred times over! Let us recognize, then, the unity we have with Jesus Christ, who desires to have a common life with us and who wills that what he has should also be ours. He wills to dwell in us, not in fiction but in fact, not in an earthly but in a spiritual way. He wills so to work in us by the power of his Holy Spirit that he is united with us more tightly than the limbs of the body.

And just as the roots of a tree thrust their substance and power into every branch, so we too derive substance and life from our Lord Jesus Christ. This is why Paul writes that our paschal lamb has been crucified and sacrificed, and that it remains for us to celebrate the festival and share in the sacrifice (1 Cor. 5:7, 8). And as in former times under the law, when the sacrifice was offered, men ate, now we also must come and take our spiritual food and refreshment in the sacrifice offered up for our redemption. We do not, it is true, consume the flesh of Jesus Christ; it does not enter via our teeth as the papists imagine. We accept the bread as a sure and unerring pledge that our Lord Jesus Christ feeds us spiritually with his body; we accept a drop of wine to show that we are spiritually nourished by his blood. Note, however, what Paul also adds here, that although under the symbols of the law it was forbidden to eat leavened bread whose dough would have been bitter, we are no longer under such shadows. We must reject the leaven of our malice, wilfulness and defilement, and we must have bread – a new lump, says Paul – which has no bitterness in it. How so? In purity and righteousness.

Therefore when we draw near to this holy table where God's Son reveals that he is our bread, that he gives himself to us for our full and complete refreshment, and wishes us to share in the sacrifice made once and for all for our salvation – when we draw near, let us be sure we do not bring with us our uncleanness and corruption, so as to wallow in them. Let us turn from them and seek to be wholly cleansed, that Jesus Christ might acknowledge us as members of his body, and that by this means we might partake of his life.

We will benefit from this holy Supper here made ready, if by it we are led to the death and passion of our Lord Jesus Christ and to his resurrection, confident that in them we have assurance of life and of salvation. By the victory he won when he rose from the dead, righteousness is given to us and the gate of heaven has been opened, so that we can boldly draw near to God and present ourselves before him, knowing that he will welcome us as his children.

> Now let us cast ourselves down before the majesty of our good God, acknowledging our faults and praying that he may mercifully receive us and that we may find grace in his sight, undeserving though we are. And may we come not only to receive pardon for the sins which we have already committed, but to be freed from all the flaws and miseries of our flesh, until he clothes us again with that perfect holiness to which he daily exhorts us.

ANNEXE

A SERMON ON THE ASCENSION

And when he had said these things, as they watched he was lifted up, and a cloud hid him from their sight. [10] *And while they were gazing into heaven as he went, behold, two men appeared before them in white robes,* [11] *and said, 'Men of Galilee, why do you stand looking up to heaven? This Jesus, who was taken up from you into heaven, will come in the same way as you saw him go.'*

(Acts 1:9-11)[1]

Our task is to explain what Luke says concerning the apostles, who saw our Lord ascend into heaven. It is not enough for us simply to know the story. We must note that what Luke describes here is one of the main articles of our faith. The articles of our faith are by no means unimportant: they are essential to salvation.

Now our Lord's ascension will be profitable to us only if we are sure that it really happened. Accordingly Luke relates that the apostles saw him ascend, and he adds that they remained standing

[1] This is the last of four sermons on the ascension (Acts 1:1-11), preached in 1549 and thus predating the sermons on Christ's death and resurrection. They were included in the Badius edition of *Plusieurs sermons* (1558). French text in *CO* 48: 614-22.

there until they were told to stay no longer, but to return to Jerusalem to exercise their ministry as they had been commanded – indeed, to the very last day (Acts 1:8). Luke thus records our Lord's ascension so that it should not be called into question. True, Scripture says, 'Blessed are those who believe and who have not seen' (John 20:29). We ought, then, to believe in the ascension more than if we had witnessed it, but since the apostles saw it and told us of it, we should be in no doubt.

We turn now to what Luke writes: *A cloud took him from their sight.* We might perhaps ask why heaven did not open, allowing the apostles to behold his exalted rank and glory. There is a good reason why the cloud obscured their sight. Our Lord has the measure of us: it is right that we should be held in check in order to correct our haughty spirits. If the apostles had been able to gaze into heaven itself, we would have had cause to swell with pride, as we are only too prone to do. We are so quick to wander at will and to throw off all restraint, to know God's secrets, and especially those he wishes to keep hidden from us. It was thus necessary that the cloud should come down before them. Thus we are taught of our need to be humble; we must not in our arrogance seek to climb higher than the heavens and to delve into God's works. Such is the lesson which this passage teaches.

We are told that *two angels appeared to them*, although Luke calls them 'men', which is how Scripture usually speaks of them. For according as angels are spiritual in nature, we cannot see them unless they show themselves in some visible form. That is why from the very first our Lord willed that they should appear as men, though always displaying some sign to prove that they were angels. If we knew them only as mortal men we would not give them the honour they deserved, and that would lessen the understanding we needed to accept their message as trustworthy. Hence God always placed some mark upon them so that men might recognize them. They are therefore said to be *clothed in white robes.* Similarly, when Jesus Christ rose from the dead, angels appeared in white garments (John 20:12). Our Lord intended that men should receive them with reverence, should listen to what they said and should banish all doubt.

It is important, however, that we notice each detail; not one is overlooked. God wants nothing to be omitted, for we know that his wisdom extends everywhere and is infinite. Furthermore, if the angels possess a certain majesty when they appear to men, what will it be like when God appears in his glory? The brilliance of the majesty of his glory is not merely like the brightness of the sun; it is like the brightness of one hundred thousand suns, supposing they existed in the world. So if angels are to be highly esteemed and reverenced, we must be careful that when God's majesty is spoken of or when it is the object of our thoughts, we must greatly revere it, conscious that we are nothing and that all majesty resides in him. This, then, is what is meant by the majesty of the angels – yes, even if they only appear in human form.

We turn now to what the angels say: *'Men of Galilee, why do you stand looking up to heaven?'* It is generally thought that the apostles were called Galileans as a term of reproach, for Galileans were not well regarded by men. According to those who hold this opinion, it is as if the angels said to the apostles, 'You poor deluded souls, do you not see that he will return in the same way as he ascended into heaven?' That, however, is not the sense in which we think the word is to be taken. The angels called them Galileans simply because that was what they were held to be. Jesus Christ himself was called this (Matt. 26:69), and when men tried to accuse the disciples of being followers of his, they asked, 'Are you not Galileans also?' (Mark 14:70; Luke 22:59). And after the death of Jesus Christ this was the word which the wicked used, as was the case with that evil man, Julian the Apostate, who, on the point of death, cried, 'You have conquered me, O Galilean!', thus cursing and deriding him, knowing that he had been defeated.[1] The apostles were therefore called Galileans, since they were thought to come from there.

Still, the angels had every reason to reprove them, for the apostles well knew that our Lord was to ascend to heaven. He had foretold it many times, and had even said, 'It is expedient for you that I go away, for if I do not, the Comforter will not come to you; but if I go, I will send him to you' (John 16:7). They must thus have forgotten this, since they remained standing, looking up to heaven to see what might result. As I said, it was necessary for him to go away. He had told them that he was to reign and that in the meantime they were to serve him on earth. He had also told them in advance that he would appear before God his Father to intercede for the faithful. They, however, showed how little they retained of what they had been taught so many times. Their ignorance should serve us as a warning: this was said not only for their sake but for ours.

Take note, then, of what the angels said, so that we may learn the benefits which come to us from our Lord's ascension. 'He will return,' they said, 'just as you saw him ascend.' This demonstrates that we are not to look for Jesus Christ here below, except when he comes to judge the whole world. When now we seek him, it has to be by faith – faith which surpasses all human understanding. That is the first lesson of this verse; it deserves our close attention.

Now because our natural tendency is always to drift downward, it is hard for us not to give way to superstition when mention is made of our Lord's ascension. Sure enough, we know what happened. Although he ascended into heaven, and although it was

[1] Julian, nephew of Constantine I, although raised a Christian, sought, as Emperor, to reimpose paganism as the official cult. The move was reversed following his death in 363 A.D.

said that he would return in the same way as he was seen to go, those who called themselves Christians did not cease to look for him on earth. How is it that men looked for him in the bread and wine, and have tried to lock him up in a cupboard, to carry him here and there and to play with him as with a doll?[1] Why do such superstitions exist, if not because our nature always tends downward like a stone? And when I say 'downward', I mean that we try to drag God down too, together with all that we know about him. We want him to be exactly like us!

Experience, then, teaches us that people always wanted to have Jesus Christ with them in the flesh. The angels, on the contrary, sought to rid us of such speculative notions, saying, 'Men of Galilee, why do you stand looking up to heaven?' Naturally when we seek our Lord we must lift our minds up to heaven, but we must not seek him according to our own intelligence and reasoning: faith must now have priority. Do we not know that faith surpasses all human understanding? It is not an ability we obtain by inheritance; it is a gift which God bestows when he corrects our nature. We must therefore seek Jesus Christ not with our eyes, our ears, our feet or hands; faith must make up for what we lack. Accordingly once we understand this verse we will be amply armed against the fantasies found everywhere in popery, where men say of a piece of bread, 'This is God', and where they think that he can be packed away like a doll. We will be amply armed, I say, against them, when we realize that Scripture tells us not to seek according to human understanding, but solely by faith.

We are further exhorted not to let our superstitions have free rein, or think that we can have God with us in bodily form. And since this is a fault which has always been true of men, we ought

[1] The initial reference is to the Roman Catholic doctrine of transubstantiation, whereby the eucharistic bread and wine are said to become the body and blood of Christ. Further references are to the tabernacle ('cupboard') in which the consecrated bread is kept, and to religious processions in which the monstrance is displayed.

to be all the more cautious. We read that the Jews said to Aaron, 'Make gods for us' (Exod. 32:1). This is how we want to have God with us, so that we can handle him and play with him. Attend, therefore, to this verse, that we may be armed against this error. For although Jesus Christ revealed himself to us and although he is our brother, we can only lay hold of him by faith. We must not picture him as we fancy him to be when he presents himself to us.

Jesus Christ has ascended up to glory. This we know. Understand, however, why he is there. Remember first what Scripture says: he did not enter a sanctuary made by the hand of man; he is in heaven above, interceding for us before God his Father (Heb. 9:24). When we presume to pray to God, we will be rejected unless Jesus Christ is there on our behalf. And because he is there he is our Intercessor, who causes our prayers to reach God and who allows us to have them answered, as if we were privileged to tell God what we have to do and to lay out our hearts before him. As we saw in the letter to the Hebrews, the high priest entered the sanctuary on behalf of all men.[1] And because Jesus Christ is now in heaven, we may be sure that he is there to intercede for us.

In entering the sanctuary the high priest bore on his head the names of the children of Israel, and on his front he wore twelve stones representing the twelve tribes of Israel, thus showing that although he entered alone, he did so on behalf of all (Exod. 28:11, 12, 21). Now since our Lord Jesus Christ has entered heaven, and since he carries us there although we are little more than senseless beasts; since he wears us on his front to show that he bears us on his heart, we should not have any doubts when we pray to God. We should be certain that our prayers will always be acceptable to God, for it is through Jesus Christ that we speak. If this had been well understood there would never have been so many

[1] Before commencing to expound Acts, Calvin had, in his Sunday sermons, preached on the letter to the Hebrews. He completed his exposition in the summer of 1549.

superstitions in popery. Why do they have so many patron saints? Why do they turn to the Virgin Mary? Because they have never understood why Jesus Christ ascended into heaven. If they had realized that he ascended to be our Intercessor, they would never have said that they were not worthy to make their requests to God, and that therefore they needed advocates. They would have realized that Jesus Christ is in heaven for our sake, and that we can have access to God without the need for patron saints and advocates. That is the first point we need to grasp.

In addition our Lord ascended into heaven so that, being at the right hand of God his Father, he should rule the world, and rule it in such a way that he always assists his faithful people and takes particular care of them. If he had remained with us, we would have given in to much worse superstition and he would not have had the power to subject all things to himself (1 Pet. 3:22). True, he might well have had that power, but we speak of him according to the order set down in his gospel. It would of course be foolish to argue about whether he might have done this or that differently, for his power is boundless. In any case it was after his resurrection that he said all power had been given to him by God (Matt. 28:18). And as our Creed says, he sits at the right hand of God the Father almighty. Does that mean that he has a seat on which he sits? No, no! He is present there as God's deputy, at his right hand. If we wished to come before God's glorious majesty we would be crushed, utterly undone. To give us access to God, however, we have Jesus Christ to whom all things are subject both in heaven and on earth (Col. 1:16). But although our Lord had complete power from eternity, we do not say that he took his seat at God's right hand until we first say that he ascended into heaven. He thus had universal supremacy after his ascension.

Note too that it is for us that he exercises this supremacy. He does not need it for himself, since with the Father he is eternal.

What then? He is at God's right hand with the nature that he took from us. This is so that we might know for certain that no harm can come to us, for we are under his protection. Yes, he may well permit us to be troubled in our flesh and to be encompassed by much misery. Yet he is always ready to extend a helping hand. We can be sure that although we may suffer for a time, it will ultimately be for our salvation. This is what we must learn when told of his ascension.

Seeing, then, that it is for our sake that he ascended and is now in heaven, there is nothing in this world we have to fear. We are, it is true, subject to much affliction so that our lot is pitiable indeed. We are more than wretched. We must not, however, be filled with fear or think only of ourselves. Rather, we should look to our Head who is already in heaven, and we should say, 'Weak though I am, there is Jesus Christ, who is powerful enough to keep me on my feet. Frail though I am, there is Jesus Christ who is my strength. Full of misery though I am, there is Jesus Christ in immortal glory. All that he has, he will give me forever, and I will share in all his blessings.'

The devil is indeed called 'the ruler of this world' (John 12:31). What then? Jesus Christ holds him in check, for he is the king of heaven and earth. The devils are up above us in the air and they wage war on us. Nevertheless Jesus Christ reigns above them, and as he is the one who has full conduct of the battle, we cannot doubt that he will give us the victory. Here on earth I am exposed to many changes which might make me lose heart. But there I see the Son of God who is my Head, and who is exempt from every change. That should be my confidence. This is how we should think of his ascension, so that we gain all we can from it.

We come to the angels' final words: '*You will see him come from heaven in the same way as you saw him go.*' Their meaning is that we should not expect him until he comes on judgment day. This should not only rid us of all superstition, but should draw us to him in heaven. We said before that we should not seek him except by faith. That being so, reflect on what Paul says to the Colossians: 'Since Jesus Christ, your Head, now dwells in heaven, and since your whole life is found in him, that is where your heart and mind should be, although here is where your body is' (cf. Col. 3:1-3). Thus, because we know that he is on high, we must learn to renounce the world if we are to be united to him. The distance between us is very great, and we would therefore be separated from him if we did not accept the means which Paul suggests – that is, we must mortify our earthly members. Paul proceeds to list them: immorality, covetousness, greed, pride, envy and all such things (Col. 3:5). Do we want to share in the ascension? Then we must not be separated from him. And how can we be joined to him? We must mortify our earthly members and everything here below that holds us fast. Some people are given to immorality and some to vengeance; some to greed or to other evils. Now just as faith lifts us high, so too our feelings should follow, prompting us to renounce the world and all that stops us from being united to our Head.

That, then, is the explanation of the verse, 'He will come in the same way as you saw him go.' We must learn to be united to him with every impulse of our heart. It is clear from this that the angels were not speaking about how he might be clothed or any such thing, despite the many madmen who look for things that are not necessary or useful for salvation. The angels' words show that he will come in visible form, as if they meant to say, 'You grieve because your Master has been taken from your sight. Do not grieve, for you will see him return with that glorious immortality which now is his.'

The papists play their little games, craftily asserting that God is in their Mass and that they have him with them, so that they can sport with him any way they please. They say that at the judgment

Jesus Christ will come visibly and openly, but that at present he comes secretly and in hidden form. Yes, he does come to us each day. Not for nothing does Scripture say that it is God who quickens us (Eph. 2:1, 5; Col. 2:13; 1 Pet. 3:18). We also affirm that the gospel testifies to his presence, but we should note how it is he dwells with us. Paul says that it is by faith (2 Cor. 5:7; Gal. 2:20; Eph. 3:12). There is no place here, then, for our dreams and fancies. We must understand the truth as Paul states it, when he says, 'Do you not know that you are God's temple in which he dwells?' (1 Cor. 6:19; 2 Cor. 6:16). So just as God is in all things and everywhere, invisibly, so Jesus Christ imparts himself to us. And when we are joined to him, our souls are nourished by the substance of his body, even though it is in heaven. This happens through the power of faith and through the Holy Spirit. Our Lord does not descend bodily, proving how ignorant the papists are when they say he comes secretly and conceals himself under the bread and wine. Since, however, we know what this verse means, let us make good use of it.

To stop the apostles feeling deprived of our Lord's presence, the angels promised that they would see him return as they had seen him go. What advantage would it have been to us if, having come down to suffer and to die, he was to be seen no more? But because we have the promise that he will return to gather us to himself and to make us one with him, this is our consolation. These words were said not only for the apostles but for us. We should learn to be comforted by the fact that although in distance we are far apart, he will appear for our redemption.

We ought, therefore, to lift up our heads and to overcome all the trials which might come our way. It is this, in fact, which allows us to judge whether we have faith in Jesus Christ. For if we rejoice when we are told that he will return, and if we feel a real desire in our hearts for his coming, it is a sign that we have true faith in him. If, on the other hand, we fear that day and feel that, if we could, we would willingly rebuff him, this is proof of our unbelief.

We know all too well that faith among men is rare. We ought to be comforted when we learn of his coming: it is the day of our redemption, as Paul says in the eighth chapter of Romans (Rom. 8:23). There are very few, however, who feel this way. So if the message that he will return fills us with sorrow, is it not a sign that we do not hope in Jesus Christ as our Redeemer? True, our redemption was accomplished by his death, but when we are rid of this body of ours we will be rid of our bondage to sin. This is why death should be something we desire. Now because the world's redemption will not take place until the last day, we must groan as all creatures do who await that day, for they are subject to corruption because of man's sin, and long to be delivered from it (Rom. 8:21, 22). Behold, then, heaven and earth and all other created things which long for Jesus Christ to appear, that he might restore everything. Would we not feel deepest shame if we did not desire his coming more than unfeeling beasts? For we not only have the knowledge which God has given us as mortal men; we have been given spirits to help us yearn for our Lord's advent. It is therefore a true sign of unbelief if we do not desire that day. If we do not lift up our heads whenever this word is uttered, we demonstrate our lack of faith in Jesus Christ.

Besides, just as this passage brings comfort to believers, so must the wicked feel dread at the thought of his coming. And although they may scoff now, their hearts are gripped by fear because our Lord is summoning them to judgment. It is only to be expected, then, that many see Jesus Christ only as their judge, for they would not accept him as their Redeemer when God offered him to them. Many nowadays merely laugh at the idea, yet they will surely see him whom they pierced (Zech. 12:10; John 19:37; Rev. 1:7).

There are some today who, when told about the judgment, will answer: 'Oh well, we will see him, but first let him come!' They are like those who last Wednesday scoffed at me here. Not content to be worthless fellows and to deride God in the taverns, they come into this place and make a show of their godlessness and insolence, behaving like brazen harlots from the bordello! So they come to mock God and his word in God's own church and in the presence of believers. Do they mock now? They will surely see, I say again, the one whom them pierced.[1]

For he will come; he will come! He did not ascend into heaven to allow the wicked to deride him without exacting retribution. He has a register in which he notes all their mockery. If they are not willing to be called to account, they must of necessity receive the judgment along with the devils, who are their brothers and their fathers.

This message is given to us for our instruction. Let us therefore learn to humble ourselves, early and soon, and to do homage to Jesus Christ. Since he is the ruler of the angels who obey him, let us keep them company by doing the same. And since we are assured that he stands before God on our behalf, let us not be afraid to pray to him. May we be comforted if now we suffer many hardships, and let us await that day of God in which the Lord Jesus has promised to come and to unite us to himself.

> Following this holy teaching, let us cast ourselves down before the face of our good God, acknowledging our faults and praying that he may not leave us to slumber, but may awaken us and unite us to his Son. And since we have been called to know him, may he give us grace continually to grow until we come to the perfection to which he calls us.

[1] On the antagonism aroused by the Reformer's work in Geneva, see above, p. 52, note 1. Some of Calvin's opponents, clearly, were not above voicing their displeasure even as he preached.

PRAYERS BEFORE AND AFTER THE SERMON

The Genevan liturgy of 1542 specified for the Sunday morning service a prayer for illumination said by the minister before the sermon, and a set prayer of intercession said after the sermon. Calvin modelled his prayer for illumination on the one which he had already used in the French church of Strasbourg. The intercessory prayer followed the brief extempore prayer with which he concluded his sermons, and was introduced by the words 'Thus we will all say …' (Texts in *CO* 23: 741–42; 6: 175–78.)

PRAYER FOR ILLUMINATION

Let us call upon our good God and Father, since all fullness of wisdom and light is found in him, mercifully to enlighten us by his Holy Spirit in the true understanding of his word, and to give us grace to receive it in true fear and humility. May we be taught by his word to place our trust only in him and to serve and honour him as we ought, so that we may glorify his holy name in all our living, and edify our neighbour by our good example, rendering to God the love and obedience which faithful servants owe their masters, and children their parents, since it has pleased him graciously to receive us among the number of his servants and children.

PRAYER OF INTERCESSION

Almighty God and heavenly Father, you have promised to hear and answer our requests which we make to you in the name of your beloved Son, Jesus Christ our Lord. We are further taught by him and his apostles to gather together in his name, with the promise that he will be among us and will intercede for us before you, that we may receive and obtain all things on which we are agreed on earth.

You bid us pray, first, for those whom you have set up over us, our leaders and governors; and next, for the needs of all your people, and of all men everywhere. Therefore, trusting in your holy truth and in your promise, being assembled here before you in Jesus' name, we lovingly beseech you, our God and Father, in your infinite mercy freely to pardon our transgressions, and so to lift our thoughts and desires to you that we may earnestly call upon you according to your good will and pleasure.

We therefore pray, heavenly Father, for all princes and lords, your servants to whom you have committed the rule of justice. Most particularly do we pray for the rulers of this city, that you will clothe them with your Spirit, who alone is gracious and sovereign, and daily increase his gifts in them, that they, acknowledging your Son Jesus Christ to be King of kings and Lord of lords, with full power in heaven and on earth, may seek to serve him and exalt his reign in all their dominions, and may according to your will guide and govern their subjects, who are the work of your hands and the sheep of your pasture. And may we, your people, here and everywhere, being kept in peace and tranquillity, serve you in holiness and righteousness; and, free from the fear of our enemies, may we give you praise all our days.

We pray also, true Father and Saviour, for all whom you have appointed to be pastors to your people, who have the care of souls and the stewardship of your holy gospel. May you lead and direct them by your Holy Spirit, that they may be found faithful and true ministers of your glory, always striving to bring home the erring and wayward sheep to the Lord Jesus Christ, our chief Shepherd and supreme Bishop, that they may daily prosper and grow in him in all righteousness and holiness. Grant, moreover, that all churches may be delivered from the mouths of ravenous wolves and hirelings, who follow their own designs and ambitions and who have no care for the honour of your holy name and the welfare of your flock.

Next we pray, most gracious God and merciful Father, for all men generally. Since you desire all men to acknowledge you as Saviour of the world, through the redemption won by our Lord Jesus Christ, may those who do not know him, being in darkness and captive to ignorance and error—may they by the light of your Holy Spirit and the preaching of your gospel be led into the way of salvation, which is to know you, the only true God, and Jesus Christ whom you have sent. May those whom you have already visited with your grace and enlightened by the knowledge of your word, grow in all goodness, enriched by your spiritual blessing, so that together we may all worship you with heart and voice, giving honour and homage to Christ, our Master, King and Lawgiver.

Likewise, O God of all comfort, we commend to you all whom you visit and chastise with cross and tribulation, whether it be through poverty or prison, sickness or exile, or affliction of body or mind. May you make known to them your fatherly love, and assure them that their chastisement is for amendment of life.

And may they with willing heart turn to you and, having turned, receive your comfort, being delivered from every distress.

Finally, O God and Father, grant also that we, who are gathered here in Jesus' name to hear his Word, may, without dissembling or hypocrisy, acknowledge that by nature we are lost, that we deserve your punishment and daily heap up condemnation to ourselves by our wretched and unruly lives. Help us to see that in us there is nothing good, and that flesh and blood can never inherit your kingdom. May we gladly and with steadfast trust submit to our Lord Jesus Christ, our only Saviour and Redeemer. And may he so live in us that, our old Adam being put to death, we may rise to a new and better life, to the praise and glory of your name.

INDEX OF SCRIPTURE REFERENCES

PSALMS (CONT'D)

PROVERBS

ISAIAH

JEREMIAH

EZEKIEL

DANIEL

JOEL

ZECHARIAH

MALACHI

MATTHEW

MARK

GENERAL INDEX

Other John Calvin titles translated by Robert White and published by the Trust

Sermons on 1 Timothy

ISBN: 978 1 84871 700 3, Clothbound, 804pp.

Sermons on 2 Timothy

ISBN: 978 1 84871 840 1, Clothbound, 488pp.

Sermons on Titus

ISBN: 978 1 84871 569 1, Clothbound, 312pp.

Sermons on the Beatitudes:
Five Sermons from the 'Gospel Harmony'
Delivered in Geneva in 1560

ISBN: 978 0 85151 934 0, Clothbound, 128pp.

Songs of the Nativity:
Selected Sermons on Luke 1 & 2

ISBN: 978 1 84871 010 8, Clothbound, 280pp.

A Guide to Christian Living[1]

ISBN: 978 1 84871 040 5, Soft cover gift edition, 168pp.

Faith Unfeigned: Four Sermons Concerning Matters Most Useful for the Present Time, with a Brief Exposition of Psalm 87

ISBN: 978 1 84871 086 3, Clothbound, 208pp.

The Institutes of the Christian Religion: A New Translation of the 1541 Edition

ISBN: 978 1 84871 463 2, Clothbound, 920pp.

[1] Also known as *The Golden Booklet of the True Christian Life*.

Some other Calvin titles
published by the Trust

Knowing God and Ourselves:
Reading Calvin's Institutes Devotionally
David B. Calhoun

ISBN: 978 1 84871 718 3, Clothbound, 360pp.

Commentary on the Psalms
John Calvin
Abridged into One Volume by David C. Searle

ISBN: 978 1 84871 031 3, Clothbound, 684pp.

Calvin's Wisdom
An Anthology Alphabetically Arranged
J. Graham Miller

ISBN: 978 0 85151 624 0, Clothbound, 424pp.

Letters of John Calvin
With a Biographical Introduction

'This is one of my favourite books. My paperback copy is highlighted, underlined, and falling apart from constant use. Students of Calvin, as well as pastors and serious Christians, will enjoy these letters. I'm thrilled that Banner of Truth has reissued this classic in a new cloth binding.' — Kevin DeYoung

ISBN: 978 1 84871 843 2, Clothbound, 320pp.

ABOUT THE PUBLISHER

THE Banner of Truth Trust originated in 1957 in London. The founders believed that much of the best literature of historic Christianity had been allowed to fall into oblivion and that, under God, its recovery could well lead not only to a strengthening of the church, but to true revival.

Inter-denominational in vision, this publishing work is now international, and our lists include a number of contemporary authors along with classics from the past. The translation of these books into many languages is encouraged.

A monthly magazine, *The Banner of Truth,* is also published. More information about this and all our publications can be found on our website or supplied by either of the offices below.

THE BANNER OF TRUTH TRUST

3 Murrayfield Road
Edinburgh, EH12 6EL
UK

PO Box 621, Carlisle,
Pennsylvania 17013,
USA

banneroftruth.org